STRUCTURED
On-the-Job
TRAINING

**A Publication in
the Berrett-Koehler
Organizational
Performance
Series**

*Richard A. Swanson &
Barbara L. Swanson,
Series Editors*

STRUCTURED
On-the-Job
TRAINING

Unleashing Employee Expertise In The Workplace

RONALD L. JACOBS
&
MICHAEL J. JONES

Berrett-Koehler Publishers
San Francisco

Berrett-Koehler Publishers, Inc.
155 Montgomery Street
San Francisco, CA 94104-4109
Tel: 415-288-0260   Fax: 415-362-2512

Ordering Information

Individual sales. Berrett-Koehler publications are available through most bookstores. They can also be ordered direct from Berrett-Koehler at the address above.

Quantity sales. Special discounts are available on quantity purchases by corporations, associations, and others. For details, contact the "Special Sales Department" at the Berrett-Koehler address above.

Orders for college textbook/course adoption use. Please contact Berrett-Koehler Publishers at the address above.

Orders by U.S. trade bookstores and wholesalers. Please contact Publishers Group West, 4065 Hollis Street, Box 8843, Emeryville, CA 94662; 510-658-3453; 1-800-788-3123; Fax: 510-658-1834

Printed in the United States of America

 Printed on acid-free and recycled paper that meets or exceeds the strictest state and U.S. guidelines for recycled paper (85% recycled waste, including 15% postconsumer waste).

Library of Congress Cataloging-in-Publication Data

Jacobs, Ronald L.
   Structured on-the-job training : unleashing employee expertise in the workplace / Ronald L. Jacobs, Michael J. Jones.

   p. cm.

   Includes bibliographical references and index.

   ISBN 1-881052-20-6 (alk. paper)

   1. Employees—Training of. 2. Employees—Training of—Evaluation.

I. Jones, Michael J.   II. Title.
HF5549.5.T7J25 1994   94-37973
658.3'1243—dc20   CIP

First Edition
99   98   97   96   95   10 9 8 7 6 5 4 3 2

Produced by: Mary Carman Barbosa
Cover design: Robb Pawlak

*This book is dedicated to our parents,
who, in their own ways,
taught us much about learning—
not in the context of the workplace
but in the context of life itself.
It is also dedicated to our respective sons:
Dustin, Eric, Jonathan,
and the newest arrival, Daniel.*

CONTENTS

PREFACE

ALMOST ALL EMPLOYEES have experienced some form of on-the-job training (OJT) in their careers, regardless of job level or type of organization. Few, if any, training programs in a setting away from the job can present all areas of knowledge and skill effectively. In a practical sense, OJT helps employees to bridge the gap between learning and making use of what was learned. And, OJT offers the potential benefit that some useful work might even be accomplished during the training period.

Carnevale and Gainer (1989) estimate the following about the use of OJT in organizations:

❏ Eighty to 90 percent of an employee's job knowledge and skills will probably be learned through OJT.

❏ Organizations will spend three times more per employee for OJT than for off-the-job training, even if there is no designated budget item for OJT.

❏ Up to one-third of an employee's first-year salary is devoted to OJT costs.

Unfortunately, in spite of the frequency of OJT programs, most are unplanned and thus ineffective. Expediency is often the major reason for using OJT, and the likely consequences of its use are not considered. In the eyes of many managers, OJT has few or no costs and can be implemented quickly and easily. The training process is often left to other employees who, while they may know their jobs, are relatively unskilled as trainers. Such an informal approach is often the major argument made against the use of OJT. As a result, many organizations rely on off-the-job training without considering its suitability for the learning task at hand.

In the past few years, increasing numbers of managers and human resource development (HRD) professionals have come to appreciate two basic truths about the training that occurs in their organizations: First—

Training programs have a strategic role in organizations.

The new economy, which demands increased flexibility in production and service delivery, use of advanced technologies, and increased responsiveness to customers' needs, has made employee know-how or expertise a strategic necessity. High-performing and successful organizations depend on employees who can perform complex tasks, such as solving problems and making decisions. But as tasks have become increasingly complex, they have also been subject to constant change. Thus, the demand for employee expertise and the accompanying need to meet changing expertise requirements have placed greater emphasis on training programs that meet the specific business needs of the organization. Second—

OJT does not have to be ineffective.

In fact, new forms of OJT have been developed during the past decade that combine the relative effectiveness of off-the-job training with the inherent efficiency and relevance of OJT. We call this improved form of OJT *structured OJT*. We use the term *structured* to distinguish it from OJT that is essentially unplanned or unstructured. Given the same degree of planning and forethought, structured OJT can be as effective as any other training approach.

These two basic truths have done much to promote the present level of interest in structured OJT. Despite this interest, few contemporary resources explain how to ensure the effectiveness of OJT. While structured OJT has many features in common with other forms of structured training, it is distinct in other respects. For example, it emphasizes one-on-one contact between experienced and novice employees as the primary means of conveying training content. By concentrating on structured OJT, this book addresses an important need in the literature on management and human resource development.

Specifically, this book provides a comprehensive guide to the design, delivery, and evaluation of structured OJT. Its underlying goal is to improve the training approaches currently used to develop employee expertise in the workplace. Once developed, this expertise can be unleashed or made available to help solve problems for the benefit of organizations and individuals alike. To achieve this goal, we tap principles drawn from sound theory and proven professional practice. Useful theory comes from sound practice, and sound practice produces predictable and consistent results—the same ends that managers in organizations have for their business processes.

A system view of structured OJT is the cornerstone of our approach. A system view ensures that structured OJT is understood in the same way that organizations are understood. Both OJT and organizations must be considered as dynamic systems that have their own sets of inputs, processes, and outputs. System designers are often concerned with how systems work together, and the same concern applies to structured OJT. Structured OJT as a training system comes into direct contact with another system, the work system. How organizations reconcile training and working when structured OJT is used is an issue of primary importance.

The recent advances in OJT could not have been made without the efforts of the various paid and volunteer government officials, organization managers, and industrial trainers who pioneered the use of OJT in the first and second world wars. The contributions of individuals involved in the Training Within Industry programs during World War II are particularly important. These individuals promoted views on training, employee expertise, and organizational change that still have much relevance today.

We seek to build on these past efforts brought about at times of great national peril to meet a challenge of a different sort today: to survive economically in an increasingly global marketplace.

Plan of the Book

The eleven chapters of the book are grouped into three parts. Part One, Meeting the Demand for Employee Expertise, provides a rationale for the use of structured OJT and a framework for understanding it. Chapter One introduces the notion of employee expertise and shows that the need for developing such expertise effectively and efficiently has prompted much of the recent interest in structured OJT. Chapter Two defines the system view of structured OJT and discusses the features that make it different from other training approaches.

Part Two, Designing, Delivering, and Evaluating Structured OJT, describes the steps involved in developing structured OJT. Chapter Three examines the four ways of using structured

OJT and shows how one decides whether to use structured OJT for a given task. Chapter Four discusses task analysis in the preparation of structured OJT modules. Chapter Five covers the selection, training, and management of structured OJT trainers. Chapter Six presents the preparation of structured OJT modules. Chapters Seven and Eight describe the delivery process. And Chapter Nine discusses the evaluation and troubleshooting of structured OJT programs. Some chapters include checklists, summary lists, or examples to guide readers through the steps involved.

Part Three, Using Structured OJT, addresses the implementation of structured OJT. Chapter Ten presents the components of a change management process that can be used to implement structured OJT pilot programs. It also examines the benefits associated with the use of structured OJT and issues involved in its use. Chapter Eleven calls for the development of an organizational culture of expertise based on the use of structured OJT and other training approaches that promote continuous learning.

Acknowledgments

This book could never have been written without the interest and support of the numerous organizations with which we have consulted or that have shared their practices with us during the past several years. Our ideas about structured OJT have been formed largely from our contacts with them. We especially want to recognize the following organizations: American Electric Power, Bank One Services Corporation, Capital City Products (now a part of Karlshamns USA, Inc.), Inland/Fisher-Guide Division of General Motors, Kenworth Truck Company, KLM Royal Dutch Airlines, Nationwide Insurance Companies, and PACCAR, Inc.

We also acknowledge the contributions of our consulting

editor, Richard A. Swanson. Throughout the process, he has been a patient and understanding friend—and one of our toughest critics. Dick's insightful feedback and comments have challenged us to produce the best book that we could. Any contribution that this book makes to the management and human resource development literature is a tribute to Dick's involvement in the writing process.

Finally, we acknowledge the support of our families, who for the past two years or so have heard about "the book" more often than they wish to count. They have taught us that the only thing more difficult than writing a book is watching someone else do it. To them all, we say thank you for being there for us.

Columbus, Ohio   Ronald L. Jacobs
November 1994   Michael J. Jones

PART ONE

Meeting the Demand
for Employee Expertise

Part One argues that developing the expertise of employees is one of the most challenging issues for managers. The proved efficiency and effectiveness of structured OJT makes it especially suitable for developing employee expertise. Most other forms of training that occur in the job setting are essentially unstructured in nature. Part One introduces the system view of structured OJT, which serves as our framework for explaining this training that occurs in the job setting.

C H A P T E R 1

The Challenge of Developing Employee Expertise

THE PRIMARY GOAL of this book is to provide a practical guide to developing employee expertise. It seems important to examine why structured OJT has attracted increasing interest among managers and human resource development (HRD) professionals. Thus, while presenting the rationale for the book as a whole, this first chapter addresses:

❑ Employee expertise and the situations in the new economy that affect expertise
❑ How organizations develop employee expertise through training
❑ Issues that have prompted the recent interest in structured OJT.

Expertise in the New Economy

Most people have faced the challenge of learning new knowledge and skills as part of their job. Training programs are designed to make this learning easier and less threatening.

Yet training is not meant to benefit individual employees only. The organization expects benefits from employees' training. In fact, training helps to ensure that employees can do what the organization asks of them. Thus, we say that training is ultimately about the issue of developing employee expertise.

Expertise is what experts know and can do. Experts are the individuals who are most capable in specific areas of human endeavor. History has seen a great variety of experts: nomadic hunters who fashioned hunting tools from pieces of flint; mathematicians who planned the Egyptian pyramids; Renaissance artists who represented three dimensions in their paintings; eighteenth-century craftsmen who manufactured precision machine tools; managers today who devise strategic plans to guide the future of their organizations. Without the expertise of skilled persons, it is unlikely that our civilization could have advanced in the way that it has over the millennia.

While expertise has been important for human progress, it is particularly important in contemporary organizations. The new economy demands increased flexibility in production and service delivery, improved use of advanced technologies, and increased responsiveness to the requirements of customers, and these demands have made expertise more highly prized than ever before (Carnevale, 1991). Drawing on the results of a four-year study, Kotter and Heskett (1992) suggest that the competitiveness of many organizations is determined largely by the knowledge, skills, and attitudes of the people in them. Peter Drucker (1993) states that knowledge is the primary resource for organizations in the present postcapitalist society.

Organizations must transform themselves if they are to become more competitive, and the know-how of individual employees has become critical for ensuring the success of the transformation process. More than ever before, high-performing and successful organizations depend on employees who can perform complex job tasks, such as solving problems and making decisions. But employees can perform complex tasks only if they possess high levels of task knowledge and skills—that is, expertise. Thus, when individual employees possess higher levels of expertise in more areas of their jobs, the organization as a whole is more able to respond effectively to the challenges that it may face.

The reality of contemporary organizations is that most employees are being asked to acquire expertise rapidly and continuously without undue interference in the ongoing work of their organization. All too often, the knowledge and skills required to perform well shift dramatically just as employees have come to feel comfortable with current ways. Customer service representatives—a function that appears, in various forms, in many organizations—have been especially prone to sudden changes in their job requirements. And when a new inventory management system is installed, a large portion of the knowledge and skills associated with the old system is no longer required.

In contrast to an organization's other resources, such as cash and equipment, expertise is not concrete. One cannot see it or reach out and touch it. Nevertheless, expertise is often more central to an organization than its tangible resources. At the same time, the effects of expertise are clearly observable. When employees use their knowledge and skills to perform some part of their job, their efforts produce a range of outcomes.

As we have stated, the people who possess the highest levels of knowledge and skill are called *experts*. By definition, experts achieve the most valuable outcomes. People whose outcomes are less valuable or who produce no outcomes can be assumed to have lower levels of knowledge and skills. These individuals are considered *novices*, or beginners. Chi, Glaser, and Farr (1988) say that, in contrast to novices, experts possess an organized body of conceptual and procedural knowledge that they can access readily and use when necessary.

Being an expert means that a person can use his or her high level of knowledge and skills in practical ways. That is the essential nature of expertise. The training certificates of a skilled professional—say, an auto mechanic or a physician—simply mean that he or she has completed the educational requirements necessary for doing the job. For a customer, the certificates signify that the jobholder has the potential for providing effective service. But the certificates do not guarantee that the mechanic or physician knows how to use the information that he or she has acquired or that he or she can take the appropriate actions in specific instances. From the customer's perspective, determining whether the professional is an expert depends on how the vehicle functions after the repair and how fast the patient recovers after the diagnosis and treatment.

Thus, expertise almost always refers to the ability to use knowledge and skills to achieve outcomes that have value to someone else. Yet, *expert* and *novice* are usually relative notions. Gilbert (1978) states that individuals who demonstrate exemplary performance or the historically best levels of performance while incurring the lowest costs in doing their jobs always seem to emerge in organizations. Therefore, we say that the outcomes achieved by experts are exemplary, but we recognize that *exemplary* is a standard that can change over time. This fact is seen most dramatically in organizations that have undergone a major downsizing. When experts leave an organization for one reason or another, other employees naturally move up to become the new experts, even if they cannot achieve outcomes equal to those of the persons who have just departed.

Employee expertise in an organization is subject to continuous change. Six highly interrelated situations affect employee expertise: new hires, job promotion, job rotation and transfer, continuous improvement efforts, multiskilling, and technology. While these situations have always been with us, they occur today with greater frequency, and their impact on organizational performance is potentially more crucial than it has been in the past.

New Hires

As entrants into the organization, new hires have always required extra organizational attention to develop their expertise. Regardless of academic background or previous work experience, the new hire should be aware of the organization's policies, culture, and mission; understand the goals and requirements of his or her work area; and use specific areas of knowledge, skills, and attitudes to do his or her job. These are all areas of expertise that the new employee should develop.

Since fewer organizations seem to be hiring large numbers of new hires, it might seem that this situation would affect employee expertise less than others. However, recent hiring patterns have complicated the matter. Instead of relying on permanent employees, many organizations are now bringing in large numbers of part-time and temporary employees. The Bureau of Labor Statistics recently estimated that 25 percent of the workforce is composed of part-time or temporary employees. The unique expertise needs of part-time and temporary new hires presents organizations with new challenges in this regard. After all, temporary employees are expected to perform at the same levels as permanent employees.

Job Promotion

Job promotion is another common situation that affects the collective expertise of organizations. When employees are given new roles or their status is upgraded, they invariably need to acquire new areas of expertise. It will take some time before these employees know and can do everything necessary in order to perform at high levels in their new job. Once the initial elation of the promotion passes, these employees often feel much discomfort and uncertainty.

The effects of job promotion on skilled technical employees who are promoted to supervisory positions is particularly evident. In their new role, these employees discover that they must perform tasks representing totally new areas of expertise, such as planning the work of others, providing coaching and counseling, and conducting feedback sessions. These demands often cause some to wonder whether they want to keep their new job or return to the relative comfort of their previous job.

Job Rotation and Transfers

Job rotation and transfers move employees into different roles or functional areas. The new assignment can be either short-term or permanent, depending on the intent of the move. Many organizations use job rotation and transfers as planned parts of the career development process. These experiences invariably place new demands on employees' expertise.

The challenge for organizations is to help these employees to achieve their individual goals by giving them access to new career opportunities whenever possible, while at the same time making certain that the movement of employees around the organization does not unduly disrupt its collective expertise.

Continuous Improvement Efforts

Employee expertise also changes as a result of continuous improvement efforts. When teams of employees get together to improve the way in which the work is done, they often come up with recommendations for change. These recommendations can involve the simplification of job tasks, use of a new tool, elimination of redundant steps in a work process, or some combination of them all. When these recommendations are enacted, changes in employee expertise can be expected.

Multiskilling

When the continuous improvement process suggests ways of making work more efficient, it often means that employees' responsibilities must broaden or that they must become multiskilled (Jones & Jacobs, 1994). Many managers find that multiskilled employees enable them to reduce costs, improve productivity, and enrich employees' jobs. Corporate downsizing has also increased the need for employees to become multiskilled.

Multiskilling makes it possible for employees to share jobs or to take over for each other when work conditions permit this to be done. Multiskilling can be an effective way of increasing efficiency and productivity, but many employees require new expertise in order to perform the additional tasks expected of them. How to acquire expertise in new tasks without lessening the individual's ability to perform present tasks remains a challenge.

Technology

Possibly the single most pervasive force affecting the expertise of organizations is technology. Technology takes many forms: using a laptop computer to calculate insurance needs, managing an automated inventory control system, or operating an industrial robot on a production line. Nearly every employee has already faced or in the future will face changes in his or her job caused by the introduction of technology. In fact, many organizations are now entering their second or third generation of technological change, which means that employees must make a continuous effort to develop new areas of knowledge and skills.

In one sense, today's technology is only a new generation of work tools, no different in many respects from the tools that man used in the past. But, because recent advances in technology have already caused such dramatic changes in the way in which work is done, many employees now expect their present expertise to have a relatively short lifespan and that they will need to acquire new expertise on a continuous basis.

To summarize, the six situations just reviewed affect the relative level of employee expertise within organizations. When employee expertise is affected in a detrimental way, it often takes the organization considerable time to recover. And while employee expertise has always been subject to change, change is more common now than it has ever been in the past, and the need for new expertise has thus increased. All these factors mean that developing employee expertise in the most effective and efficient ways possible is one of today's major challenges.

Developing Expertise Through Training

Training is the primary means in which organizations develop employee expertise. In this sense, training and expertise go hand in hand. Expertise is what the most capable employees know and can do on the job, while training is the means used to communicate that knowledge and skill to others. Of course, training alone cannot make an employee into an expert. Training can only help an employee to achieve a certain level of mastery, and the employee must make an effort over time to develop expertise. But one cannot become an expert without first achieving mastery. And the best way of achieving mastery is through some form of training.

In this book, we distinguish training in organizations by the two basic locations in which it is conducted: off the job and on the job.

Off-the-Job Training

In general, off-the-job training programs provide group-based learning opportunities on a variety of topics at a site other than where the work is actually done. Off-the-job training can be conducted in an off-site training classroom near the job setting, in an adjoining facility dedicated exclusively to training, or in a corporate or private facility located far away from the job setting. In many instances, off-the-job training requires extensive travel. Training classrooms, vestibule training setups, and specially constructed training laboratories are some examples of off-the-job training sites.

Within the past thirty years or so, the use of formal off-the-job training programs has risen dramatically. Carnevale and Gainer (1989) estimated that more than $30 billion are spent for off-the-job training programs every year. Although this figure is impressive, it may not reflect the total cost of off-the-job training. Many organizations have made sizable investments in the construction of specialized training centers and campus-like facilities in which their training programs are conducted. Nor does the figure just cited include the costs of the human resource development staff who design, deliver, and manage the training programs conducted in these facilities. These expenses would undoubtedly increase the cost of off-the-job training programs.

On-the-Job Training (OJT)

Not all training occurs off-site. In fact, most learning occurs as a result of training conducted in the job setting itself (Wexley & Latham, 1991). OJT is the process in which one employee, most often the supervisor or lead person of a work area, passes job knowledge and skills to another employee (Broadwell, 1986). OJT occurs at the location in which the work is done or at least as near to the work as possible, and it is often thought of as involving both learning and doing at the same time.

Historically, OJT has always figured prominently in the acquisition of job expertise (Miller, 1987). After all, before there were off-site corporate training classrooms, the only way in which a person could reasonably expect to learn a profession or a trade was by working at the side of an experienced employee. For example, during the Middle Ages, apprentices worked with a master craftsman, who exercised considerable control over their work and socialization experiences, for long periods of time. During the latter part of the nineteenth century and the beginning of this century, supervisors and foremen used OJT to show new industrial workers how to operate production machinery.

Most discussions of OJT refer to the influential role that it played during the two world wars in this century. Interestingly, these two periods of immense national threat brought about the most important advances in the use of OJT. During World War I, Charles R. "Skipper" Allen drew on his experiences as a vocational educator to devise a four-step method of delivering OJT. Supervisors used the four steps to train civilian shipbuilders who had never before worked in an industrial environment (McCord, 1987).

While Allen's efforts were highly successful, they received little attention after the war. In fact, not until the start of World War II did a wide audience appreciate the contributions of Allen's four-step delivery process.

OJT may have received its greatest emphasis as the result of the Training Within Industry (TWI) Service, an agency of the War Manpower Commission's Bureau of Training, which was created in 1940 and discontinued in 1945 (Dooley, 1945). One of the most serious expertise shortages at the time was in skilled lens grinders and polishers of precision instruments, such as the optical instruments used on bombsights. During the first week of its existence, the TWI commissioned a study to evaluate a new way of training lens grinders. During the study, a comprehensive job analysis was conducted, and a seven-step training process based on Allen's four steps was devised. These were the seven steps:

1. Show him how to do it.
2. Explain the key points.
3. Let him watch you do it again.
4. Let him do the simple parts of the job.
5. Help him do the whole job.
6. Let him do the whole job, but watch him.
7. Put him on his own.

The lens grinder study was highly successful: Training time was reduced from the original estimate of five years to six months. Later, when the seven steps from the lens grinder study were found to be too cumbersome, Allen's original four steps were adopted as the standard for delivering job instruction training.

Building on the success of the lens grinder study, the TWI established the Job Instruction Training (JIT) program, which focused primarily on the delivery of technical skills. Possibly the most prominent aspect of JIT continues to be the job instruction card—a card that presents two sets of information:

1. How to Get Ready to Instruct

    Have a timetable. How much skill do you expect the trainee to have by what date?

    Break down the job. List the important steps. Pick out the key points. Safety is always a key point.

    Have everything ready. Do you have the right equipment? the right materials? the right supplies?

    Arrange the workplace properly. Is the workplace just as the trainee will be expected to keep it?

2. How to Instruct

    Prepare the worker. Put the trainee at ease. State the job and find out what the trainee knows about the job. Get the trainee interested in learning about the job. Place the trainee in the correct position.

    Present the operation. Tell, show, and illustrate each step in the process carefully and patiently one step at a time. Stress each key point. Instruct clearly and completely.

    Try out performance. Have the trainee perform the job, and correct errors. Have the trainee explain each key point while performing the job. Make sure that the trainee understands by asking questions and correcting errors. Continue until you are certain that the trainee has learned.

    Follow up. Put the trainee in the performance setting on his own. Assign people to be helpers along the way. Check the trainee frequently, but taper off coaching as time goes by. Praise good work and coach to correct poor work.

The job card concluded with the admonition: *If the worker hasn't learned, then the trainer hasn't taught.* The TWI Service followed up on the JIT program with others, including Job Methods Training (JMT), Job Relations Training (JRT), Union Relations Training (URT), and Program Development. All these programs emphasized the job setting as the primary location for delivery of training content.

Although the TWI Service was discontinued in 1945, the successes of its programs undoubtedly encouraged participating organizations to continue the use of OJT after the war. Recent surveys of industry training practices confirm that OJT is the training method most often used for a wide range of jobs, including skilled, semiskilled, sales, supervisory, and management positions; types of organizations; and sizes of organizations (Futrell, 1988; Churchill, Ford, & Walker, 1985; Kirkpatrick, 1985; Kondrasuk, 1979; Utgaard & Davis, 1970; Rothwell & Kazanas, 1990).

Carnevale and Gainer (1989) estimate that an employee learns 90 percent of his or her job knowledge and skills through OJT. They believe that organizations will spend three times more on OJT training for each employee than they will for off-the-job training, and they point out that most organizations have no designated budget item for OJT. Finally, up to one-third of a newly hired employee's first-year salary is devoted to the costs of OJT. These results confirm what many managers and employees know from experience: Most training takes place at the job site, not in a training classroom.

Emergence of Structured OJT

The effects of the new economy have necessarily increased the importance of training within organizations. However, while training has generally found itself in a more strategic position, this has not meant that everyone has been totally satisfied with the way in which training has been used. In fact, both managers and HRD professionals have expressed concerns about how training is carried out in their organizations (Sloman, 1989). Paradoxically, the more often training is used, the more concern seems to be expressed about it. To a large extent, the emergence of structured OJT has been the result of these concerns.

Concerns with Off-the-Job Training

At first glance, most off-the-job training programs appear to be effective, of high quality, and generally well received by trainees. By virtue of its location, an off-site training program may offer some trainees a reprieve from the pressures of the immediate job setting, which helps them to focus more intently on the training content. Nevertheless, many managers recognize that, no matter what topic is presented, off-the-job training programs can result in any one of the following problems:

❏ Employees learn what was presented in the training, but because no one else from their work area was aware of the nature of the training program, they seldom have occasion to use what they learned.

❏ Employees learn what was presented in the training, but because no one highlighted the aspects that were critical for meeting customers' needs before the training occurred, they are uncertain of the relevance of the information learned.

❏ Employees enjoy learning the content of the training programs and praise the programs after they return to their work area without realizing that what they have learned is different from what they practice on their jobs.

❏ Employees return to their work area and discover that what they learned during the training represented only a small amount of the information that they require in order to do their jobs.

❐ Employees learn what was presented in the training and achieve the desired levels of expertise, but because management fails to supply the follow-up required to sustain those new levels over time, their use of the information inevitably drops off.

As a result of these concerns, many managers have come to suspect that the goals of off-the-job training programs often contradict the organization's goals. Increasingly, training content and schedules seem unresponsive to the sponsoring organization's business needs, and training certificates take on more importance than job knowledge and skills. At the same time, many HRD professionals perceive that managers do not realize how much time is required to design effective off-the-job training programs. Nonetheless, off-the-job training programs may cost more than the value they produce for an organization.

Concerns with OJT

OJT has been subject to different concerns. While OJT has been used more often than off-the-job training, most instances of OJT are essentially informal, which means that they occur without advance planning or involvement by management. The entire training may be placed in the hands of an individual who does not know the task and who considers the training an imposition on his or her work time. Under these conditions, training takes lower priority than work, even when training might help to improve the quality of work. Most employees are forced to learn regardless of these constraints. Thus, most of the OJT programs conducted in organizations can be considered unplanned or, as Swanson and Sawzin (1975) describe them, as unstructured in nature.

Unstructured OJT occurs when trainees acquire job knowledge and skills from impromptu explanations or demonstrations by others; through trial-and-error efforts, self-motivated reading, or questioning on their own; or simply by imitating the behavior of others. Consider the comments of a newly hired nurse who received unstructured OJT from an experienced nurse. Her comments are representative of most employees who receive unstructured OJT:

> When I first came on, I was trained by another nurse at the time. We became friends, more or less. I relied on her to tell me what to do. She told me, "Do this. Don't do that. This is how I do this." Eventually, I learned what she wanted me to learn, but I found that I could learn just as well on my own. I'm not sure if I really learned what they wanted me to learn. Anyway, after a while, I just started figuring out things on my own.

Unstructured OJT has been called many things: follow Joe (or Jane) training, sink-or-swim training, sit by Nellie training, learning the ropes, do-it-yourself training, to name only a few. Anyone of working age has been subjected to this type of training at some point in his or her career and knows the frustration that it can cause. Moreover, unstructured OJT has a number of problems:

❏   The desired level of expertise is rarely, if ever, achieved, and when it is, all trainees rarely achieve the same level.

❏   The training content is often inaccurate or incomplete, or else it represents an accumulation of bad habits, misinformation, and possibly unsafe shortcuts on which employees have come to rely over time.

❑ Experienced employees are seldom able to communicate what they know in a way that others can understand.

❑ Experienced employees use different methods each time they conduct the training, and all methods are not equally effective.

❑ Many employees fear that sharing their knowledge and skills will reduce their own status as experts and possibly even threaten their job security.

Thus, while unstructured OJT occurs most often, employees seldom achieve the desired levels of expertise as a result of its use. Our own research has shown that unstructured OJT leads to increased error rates, lower productivity, and decreased training efficiency (Jacobs, 1994; Jacobs, Jones, & Neil, 1992). Perhaps the best that can be said about unstructured OJT is that, despite its problems, most employees eventually overcome the barriers that it creates and learn at least some of what they need to know. Managers often believe that they can train employees and do their own work at the same time. Unfortunately, such an arrangement does not provide the basis for a positive learning experience, nor does it make the most efficient use of organizational resources.

To summarize, off-the-job training programs are well intentioned, but they either miss the mark, or they are too far away from the performance setting to have an impact on employees' expertise. Managers can ill afford to take employees away from their jobs each time training is required or wait patiently for the programs needed to be scheduled at the convenience of someone else. Moreover, most uses of unstructured OJT are ineffective in achieving the training objectives, which inhibits the achievement of important organizational outcomes. Training should take place close to the point of job performance. At times, this means close to the customer.

Demographic projections about the future workforce and its educational characteristics complicate these concerns. Johnston and Packer (1987) assert that the need for employee training and development will become increasingly acute in the near future, in large part because a large number of individuals entering the labor market do not have the skills required for high-wage jobs. No single training approach can possibly meet the developmental needs of these diverse individuals.

The conjunction of these issues has motivated much of the recent interest in structured OJT. Although structured OJT is not a panacea, it has potential for developing employee expertise effectively and efficiently. For many organizations, the challenge today is one of surviving in an era that emphasizes the quality of products and services, cooperation between employees and management, and high efficiency (Kaufman & Jones, 1990). This book seeks to help organizations respond to these challenges through the ongoing development of employee expertise.

Conclusion

Expertise is important for most organizations that seek to meet the challenges of the new economy. In the process of helping employees to develop the expertise they require, managers and HRD professionals recognize that off-the-job training programs often do not have the desired relevance and that on-the-job training efforts are often ineffective. The interest in structured OJT has emerged in this context.

C H A P T E R 2

A System View
of Structured OJT

MUCH OF THE increased interest in structured OJT comes from its effectiveness, which is greater than that of the unstructured forms of OJT. This chapter builds an understanding of structured OJT by viewing it from a system perspective. Topics covered in this chapter include:

- ❐ The meaning of structured OJT
- ❐ The system view of structured OJT
- ❐ Two defining features of structured OJT.

The Meaning of Structured OJT

As far as can be determined, Jacobs and McGiffin (1987) make the first reference to *structured OJT* as a unique form of training. Many authors before them, including Goldstein (1974) and Connor (1983), had suggested the need for more structured forms of OJT, but they were the first to differentiate clearly from unstructured OJT. As we stated in Chapter One, OJT received a great deal of attention during both world wars, but today's efforts to improve OJT are driven by challenges of a different sort. Today, managers must find ways of combating the effects of changing market demands, advanced technologies, and lowering production and service delivery costs.

Interest in structured OJT can be confirmed by the references to it in the professional literature, such as those by Carnevale and Carnevale (1994), Martin (1991), Wehrenberg (1987), Sullivan and Miklas (1985), and Connor (1983). De Jong (1993) has described how eight organizations in the Netherlands, which ranged from banks to the national railway system, have used structured OJT for employees at a variety of organizational levels. Organization managers and human resource practitioners in the Netherlands have been especially interested in structured OJT and the related topic of learning in the workplace. Rothwell and Kazanas (1990) studied the use of structured OJT in various types of organizations. They found that most organizations, especially manufacturing organizations, were doing a substantial amount of their training through OJT, but it was unclear whether the OJT that they observed had been planned and delivered in a systematic manner.

Organizations refer to their structured OJT programs in a number of different ways, including *task training, workplace training programs, training on the job, on the job coaching*, and *planned OJT*. Absent from the literature only a few years ago, structured OJT, under one or another of its several names, is now a generally recognized form of training that is available in many organizations.

We define structured OJT as:

The planned process of developing task-level expertise by having an experienced employee train a novice employee at or near the actual work setting.

This definition makes three points clear: First, like other structured training approaches, structured OJT requires a substantial investment of time and effort before it can be used. As a planned process, structured OJT can be expected to achieve training objectives more reliably than unstructured OJT, which receives little or no advanced planning.

Second, the interaction that occurs between the individuals involved in the training occurs for the purpose of passing along expertise about specific areas or tasks. The term *tasks* refers to the discrete sets of behaviors and outcomes that characterize the jobs of all individuals, ranging from frontline employees to senior managers. Delivering task-level information on a one-on-one basis has been shown to have unique benefits over group instruction methods and self-instructional approaches that use printed materials or automated devices (Bloom, 1984). Thus, structured OJT takes full instructional advantage of this immediate level of social contact.

Third, as Table 2.1 shows, structured OJT is clearly different from the other ways of learning task-level information. Self-directed discovery assumes that the employee will be able to learn a task through information available in the work setting. The information is either put there intentionally, or it exists there as a natural part of this environment. The unstructured form of self-directed discovery can be characterized as learning by doing. False assumptions about the task and numerous errors are often the result. The structured use of self-directed discovery relies on job performance aids, electronic performance support systems, and self-paced instructional materials.

Coaching assumes that the trainee can perform some, but not all, of the task. Another employee coaches the trainee at specific points either to present unknown information or to

Table 2.1. Ways of Learning Task-Level Information On the Job

Self-Directed Discovery	Coaching	On-the-Job Training
Unstructured		
Employee learns by doing, with limited information intentionally placed in the work setting to guide learning. Employee must figure out each part of the task without assistance. False assumptions and errors are the result.	Employee learns by working alongside or nearby an experienced employee, who seldom knows exactly how or when to intervene as the task is performed.	Employee is trained by an experienced employee, whose experience as a trainer is likely to be limited and whose task expertise may also be questionable. Training content, methods, and outcomes vary across employees.
Structured		
Employee learns while doing, using information engineered into work setting to guide learning. Employee can trust the system to help make the learning easier and reduce frustration.	Employee learns by working alongside or nearby an experienced employee, who uses systematic knowledge of the task to know when and how to intervene. Training outcomes are relatively predictable.	Employee is trained by an experienced employee who has expertise as a trainer and in the task to be learned. Training content, methods, and outcomes are consistent across employees.

point out ways of improving task behaviors already learned. When coaching is unstructured, the trainee works alongside others, who—it is hoped—will somehow know when and how to intervene. When coaching sessions are structured, the trainer knows how and when to intervene during the trainee's performance of the task.

In contrast to self-directed discovery and coaching, structured OJT assumes that the trainee lacks the knowledge and skills that he or she needs in order to perform the task. Thus having the trainee perform the task while learning it can be risky. Distinguishing between self-directed discovery, coaching, and OJT can be difficult in practice. These various ways of learning task-level information are often used in combination.

Viewing Structured OJT as a System

Structured OJT differs from unstructured OJT in making use of a planned process. Carrying out the planned process with a system view helps to ensure that the training will be efficient and effective. No other theoretical framework for instruction and performance improvement can make that promise (Jacobs, 1989). The system view maintains that all natural and artificial entities are systems and that the behavior of systems is relatively predictable, which means that we can design and manage them with some confidence.

This era of unpredictable change makes the argument for systems thinking even more compelling (Senge, 1990). Patterns inevitably emerge that help us to explain present events and predict future events. For managers, systems thinking is sometimes as simple as recognizing that if you push on one side of the organization, the opposite side is likely to move, too, but in the opposite direction. Managers should use what they know about the system at hand to respond in informed ways to the reactions observed.

The system view also helps us to distinguish between the means and ends of our actions. Like many others before us, we maintain that every training approach, including structured OJT, is merely a means to an end, not an end in itself. The use of structured OJT is not the ultimate goal that we seek to achieve when we advocate the use of structured OJT. Rather, structured OJT is one way of improving organizational performance, because it develops employees' expertise. When employees have expertise, they can increase their productivity, complete projects on time, lower defect rates, or achieve other outcomes of importance. These are the outcomes that matter for organizations, and the effectiveness of structured OJT should always be judged from this perspective.

The system view has two basic implications for structured OJT. First, it says that structured OJT is a system composed of several interacting parts that work together to achieve common goals (Jacobs, 1989; Rummler & Brache, 1990). Second, it says that structured OJT should be developed and implemented systematically.

The two implications interrelate in fundamental ways. The structured OJT process guides how we put together effective structured OJT regardless of the nature of the task. And in order to improve the training with greater precision, the structured OJT should be thought of as a functioning system.

Structured OJT System

Figure 2.1 shows the training inputs, training process, and training outputs implied in the view of structured OJT as a system. It also shows that the components are affected by the organizational context in which the system exists. This perspective may be puzzling to readers who see OJT simply as a purposeful conversation between two or more employees. However, the training event is more than the social interactions. In fact, structured OJT represents the interaction of several parts that are essential for ensuring the success of the system. Some of these parts may not be apparent.

Training Inputs. The training inputs of structured OJT include the people, information, physical objects, and locations necessary to conduct the training. The first input in the system is the novice employee who lacks the necessary knowledge, skills, or attitudes needed to do the task and who is therefore the trainee. In order for the training to be effective, the *novice employee* should possess:

Figure 2.1. Structured OJT as a System

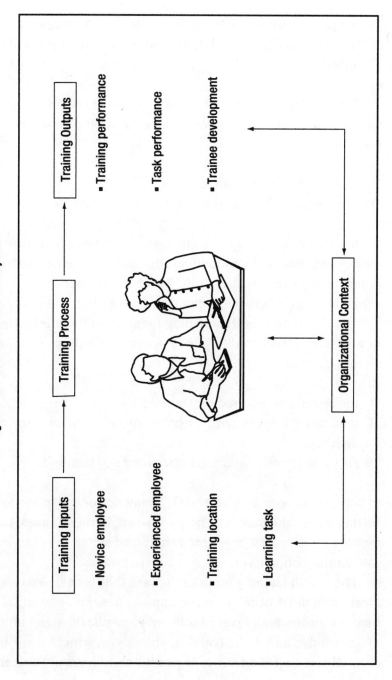

- ❏ the prerequisites needed to learn the training content
- ❏ the personality style that is best suited for the training approach.

The next input is the experienced employee who functions as the trainer. The *experienced employee* should have a combination of:

- ❏ knowledge and skills in the task
- ❏ knowledge and skills as a trainer.

We use the term *experienced employee* in preference to *expert employee* because the individual who has the most expertise is not always the best trainer. The best trainer combines expertise in the task with expertise in training.

The third input is the training location in the job setting in which the structured OJT is to occur. The *training location* should provide:

- ❏ the resources required for training
- ❏ minimal conflicts with ongoing production or service delivery
- ❏ an atmosphere conducive for training and learning.

In some instances, structured OJT may not occur in the job setting where the task is to be performed. In these cases, the training location that is selected should be suited to achieving the training objectives.

The fourth training input is the task that is to be learned. More than most other training approaches, structured OJT focuses on the task level of jobs or on similarly sized units of knowledge and skill. Training objectives, which describe the abilities that the trainee is predicted to have at the conclusion of training, are defined in terms of learning tasks. The *learning task* should be:

☐ selected as being suited for structured OJT
☐ analyzed into component behaviors
☐ related to training objectives and other important information
☐ combined with other information into a training module.

Training Process. In the process component of structured OJT, the trainer delivers the module to the trainee, who learns the content. Thus, the actions of the trainer before, during, and after he or she delivers the training to a large extent determine the effectiveness of the training. The steps of the training process include:

☐ the trainer's actions to get ready to train
☐ the trainer's actions in using the structured OJT module as intended
☐ the trainer's actions to ensure that the trainee has learned.

Training Outputs. The training outputs occur as a result of combining the training inputs during the training process. The training outputs include the ability of the novice employee to:

☐ perform the task to the level defined by the training objectives
☐ perform the task to the level required by the job
☐ achieve his or her development goals.

Logically, the primary output of any training system is the achievement of training objectives. However, the achievement of training objectives cannot be judged in isolation from the other possible outcomes of the system. Do the training objectives address the needs of the individual employee and the organization? Remember that the business needs of the organization were what motivated us to use structured OJT in the first place.

Organizational Context. Finally, as a system, structured OJT exists within a larger context. In effect, structured OJT is a system in direct contact with other, sometimes conflicting, systems, such as the work system. Thus, the various components of the structured OJT system are subject to influence from issues that emerge from the organizational context. These are some of the major issues that affect structured OJT:

❏   Business priorities facing the organization, such as reducing personnel costs, improving quality, or increasing market share

❏   The nature of ongoing change efforts, such as companywide productivity studies, process improvement programs, or safety programs

❏   Perceptions of the value of training that prevail among senior management, supervisors, and employees

❏   Contractual agreements between management and unions that prohibit some line employees from serving as trainers

❏   Alignment between the goals of training and the goals of related organizational systems

❏   Alignment between job expectations and the consequences of using experienced employees as trainers

❏   Willingness of line and staff functions to manage and maintain the structured OJT after it has been implemented.

As we note in Chapter Nine, organizational issues can often determine the success or failure of structured OJT.

Structured OJT Process

Figure 2.2 presents the second implication of the system view, namely that we need an orderly process for the design, delivery, and evaluation of structured OJT. In general, the six steps shown are the ones that allow us to put together a system in the most effective and efficient way possible. In that sense, the process shown is ideal. It often has to be adapted in practice to fit the demands of new situations. Often, the steps in the process are used iteratively, which means that two steps can occur at the same time or that steps can be repeated as learning occurs.

The structured OJT process should be considered a subset of the larger performance improvement process. As such, the structured OJT process should be developed only after a thorough analysis of the gap between present job performance and desired job performance. As we stated earlier, structured OJT is appropriate only when the existing or anticipated performance problem is caused by a lack of knowledge, skills, or attitudes. Readers unfamiliar with needs assessment or performance analysis should consult Rossett (1987), Kaufman and Zahn (1993), and Harless (1978).

The structured OJT process has six steps:

Decide whether to use structured OJT. The first step in the process is to determine whether it is appropriate to use structured OJT for the tasks at hand. To perform this step, you should have knowledge of the instructional features of structured OJT and of specific selection criteria.

Analyze the tasks to be learned. Once you have identified the learning tasks that are appropriate for structured OJT, you should analyze the tasks in order to derive the training content and outcomes. Some design processes place task analysis before the selection of training approach. We reverse the order because we assume that a task inventory is available

Figure 2.2. Structured OJT Process

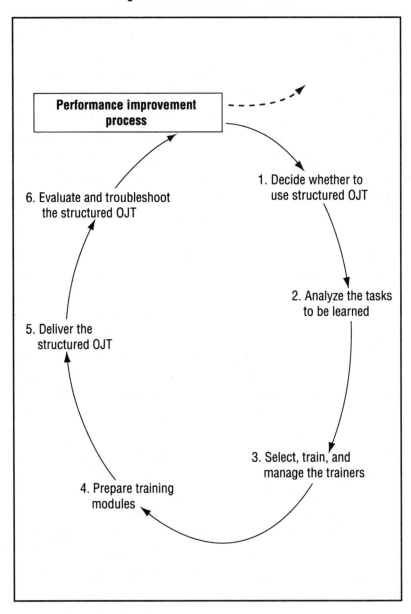

when the process begins. If it is not, job tasks should be identified before the training approach is selected.

Select, train, and manage the trainers. Structured OJT is effective only when experienced or knowledgeable employees serve as trainers. Trainers should have both task and instructional expertise. The development of trainers is often a process by itself.

Prepare training modules. The training content and other important information should be assembled into a structured OJT module. The module guides the trainer while he or she delivers the training, and the trainee uses it as a reference during the training.

Deliver the structured OJT. Before delivering the training, the trainer must do everything that he or she needs to do in order to be ready to train. Then, the trainer delivers the training in a way consistent with the type of training involved: managerial, technical, or awareness. Delivery is guided by the five basic training events:

❒ Prepare the trainee
❒ Present the training
❒ Require a response
❒ Provide feedback
❒ Evaluate performance.

How these training events are used depends on the type of training.

Evaluate and troubleshoot the structured OJT. The various outcome, process, and input components should be evaluated in light of the performance expectations. Any unanticipated effects must also be evaluated. We troubleshoot the system by matching problems and causes. This information helps us to develop suggestions for action, which can then be considered. Evaluation and troubleshooting must be continuous.

The Defining Features of Structured OJT

Most organizations use an array of training approaches. For instance, computer-based training has been emphasized in recent years. Despite the many advances in training delivery, the effectiveness of any given training approach still depends on two features: the amount of time that elapses between training events and the match between training setting and job setting.

Time Between Training Events

As Figure 2.3 shows, the time between training events can be thought of as the sum of the time between the presentation of training content (A) and the trainee's opportunity to actively respond to the content (B) and feedback from the trainer about the adequacy of the trainee's response (C). In general, a trainee learns the training content more efficiently and effectively when training events occur close together than when they are relatively spread apart in time (Wexley, 1988).

Clearly, structured OJT matches or beats most other training approaches, especially classroom-based training, in its potential to reduce the amount of time between training events. This potential is a function of the one-on-one contact that occurs during training and of the fact that training is located in the job setting. Most trainers have long known that it is important to give trainees an opportunity to use what they have learned as soon as possible. Some refer to it simply as the opportunity to learn by doing at the same time (Black & Bottenberg, 1973).

Match Between Training Setting and Job Setting

The benefits that accrue from reduced time between training events are enhanced by the potential of structured OJT to provide learning experiences that closely match or even

Figure 2.3. Effectiveness and Efficiency Increase When Delay Decreases

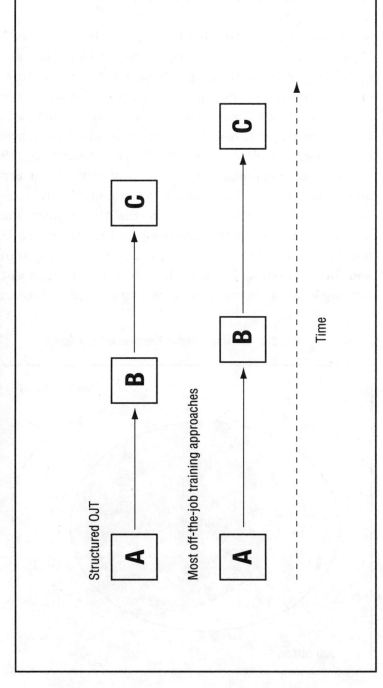

Structured OJT

Most off-the-job training approaches

Time

duplicate the behaviors that are required in the job setting. Figure 2.4 shows that the transfer of training increases as the match between the training setting and the job setting increases. Transfer of training is the process of using what one has learned in one situation in other situations, which can differ in some respects from the situation in which the learning took place (Baldwin & Ford, 1988; Broad & Newstrom, 1992).

Transfer of training is often the most critical concern of managers who send their people to training. Will trainees be able to use the knowledge and skills that they acquire on the job after attending a training program? In structured OJT, there is usually a close match between the training setting and the job setting, because the job setting is used as the training location. In many instances, structured OJT uses the

Figure 2.4. Training Transfer Requires a Close Match

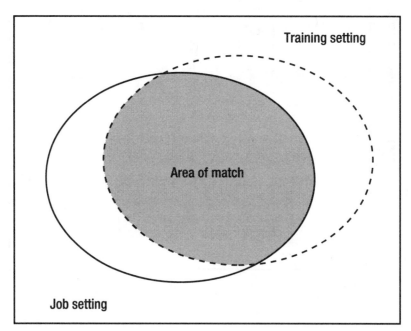

very equipment and tools that the trainee will be expected to use on the job after training. For this reason, structured OJT increases the potential for transfer of training.

Several researchers suggest that use of the job setting for learning can make a qualitative difference in the results (Hart-Landsberg, Braunger, Reder, & Cross, 1992; Brown, Collins, & Duguid, 1989). Lave and Wenger (1991) argue that context-based learning is situated, because the learning occurs in an environment that is connected to the information being presented. The information and the environment interact in ways that tend to strengthen each other.

Conclusion

Structured OJT is the planned process of developing expertise by having novice employees learn task-level information directly from experienced employees in the work setting. The system view of structured OJT has two major implications: First, structured OJT is a system in itself. Second, structured OJT should be developed and used systematically. The two defining features of structured OJT distinguish it from most other training approaches that organizations use in the work setting. Building on this understanding, the chapters that follow present the steps required to design, deliver, and evaluate structured OJT.

PART TWO

Designing, Delivering, and Evaluating Structured OJT

In this part of the book, we present the steps of the structured OJT process. The process should be thought of as part of the overall performance improvement process within the organization. The decision to engage in this process must be supported by a documented business issue of importance that is caused by employees' lack of knowledge, skills, or attitudes. If it is not, the training is likely to waste scarce organizational resources.

C H A P T E R 3

Deciding Whether to Use Structured OJT

ONE PART OF ANY DECISION to use structured OJT is becoming aware of the ways in which it can be used. Another is determining what conditions are appropriate for its use. This chapter focuses on deciding when to use structured OJT, by examining these two parts of the decision-making process:

❐ Four ways of using structured OJT
❐ Five selection factors.

Ways of Using Structured OJT

An organization can use structured OJT to present a single training program, to present training programs related to a job, to present training programs related to a work process or a set of operations, and to present a training program in combination with off-the-job training. Or, these four ways can be combined. For example, a series of structured OJT modules related to a work process can be used in combination with off-the-job training programs. Structured OJT is seldom used in isolation from other training experiences.

41

Single Training Program

Possibly the most common way of using structured OJT is as a single training program that addresses a specific set of expertise. In this way, structured OJT modules are often used strategically. That is, trainees receive training precisely when they need to learn the knowledge and skills.

For example, most employee grievances in the financial services division of a large insurance company were directed at newly promoted supervisors. The grievance process is time-consuming, disruptive, and costly to the organization. Employees' reasons for initiating grievances vary, but a performance analysis showed that many grievances were the result of supervisors' attempts to give performance feedback to subordinate employees.

To address the cost of grievances, giving subordinate feedback was removed from the existing management training curriculum and then converted into a structured OJT module. Experienced supervisors who were recognized for their ability to give effective feedback to subordinates were asked to conduct the structured OJT. Newly promoted supervisors were assigned to an experienced supervisor to receive training on this topic. The results showed that trainees were better able to demonstrate the performance feedback process after the structured OJT than trainees had been after the classroom-based training.

In a manufacturing organization, the quality of the work of employees who had received structured OJT was compared with the quality of the work of employees who had received unstructured OJT. Several inspection points on the finished product were linked to specific tasks that employees did on the production line. Work quality was assessed as number of defects made over a year's time. The results showed that, at least at one inspection point, structured OJT led to higher-quality work. In fact, the reduced defect rates saved the organization more than $20,000 in rework costs (Jacobs, 1994).

Multiple Training Programs

Structured OJT has also been used to present multiple training programs related to a job. In this way, several structured OJT modules are developed. Each module addresses a specific job competency. Together, the modules can be thought of as a training curriculum. Often, trainees progress through the modules in a specified sequence.

For example, a large regional bank uses structured OJT to give new and experienced tellers knowledge of a large number of financial products suitable for retail customers. It also uses structured OJT to train tellers in the skills needed to sell these products. As part of their job, tellers are now expected, when appropriate, to suggest and explain the products to customers. The bank reported that tellers were meeting group sales goals and that several tellers had used this experience to boost their efforts to be promoted to higher-level customer service positions within the bank.

The quality control testing laboratory of an edible oil processing company uses structured OJT to prepare newly hired lab technicians to perform eighteen basic lab tests. Lab technicians are key players in the refining process, since the results of their inspections are used to determine whether the product is ready for the next step of the process. The structured OJT was conducted by supervisors at off-peak times and after hours. Structured OJT reduced training time from twelve weeks to three weeks (Jacobs & McGiffin, 1987).

Training Programs Related to a Work Process

Increasingly, structured OJT is being used to present training related to tasks within a work process as opposed to a job. Often, the tasks related to a process are performed within one or more adjoining work areas. In this way, many employees can receive cross-training on many different tasks.

For example, a manufacturer of nutritional supplements and infant formula has streamlined the customer order process to reduce the number of employees to whom large institutional customers must be referred when their purchasing agents call to inquire about orders. Telephone sales agents, contract specialists, and account managers were trained on a core set of tasks, which included determining shipment schedules, identifying shipment locations for individual products, and calculating volume discounts. The results of structured OJT on these tasks showed that customers' inquiries were being addressed with significantly fewer telephone "bounces" than they had been before the organization adopted the process perspective.

In a manufacturing organization with union representation, structured OJT helped team members to cross-train each other on the operation, troubleshooting, and maintenance of various production and inspection equipment in their work area. The results showed that, after structured OJT, all fifteen team members could operate all the pieces of equipment in their work area within three weeks. Before training, each team member could operate only one piece of equipment, and none could use the sophisticated testing equipment used to inspect parts.

Combined with Off-the-Job Training

Finally, structured OJT has been used as a follow-up or in combination with off-the-job training programs. Such combinations recognize that group-based training can be better suited than structured OJT to achieve some training objectives, while structured OJT is better suited to achieve others.

For example, KLM Royal Dutch Airlines uses group-based training in a classroom to present the basics of customer service for newly hired cabin attendants who will serve on over-seas flights. HRD staff found that asking trainees to practice using customer service concepts on peer trainees severely limits the effectiveness of the training, even when the class-room has been designed to look like the inside of a commer-cial airliner with airline seats, kitchen bays, service trolleys, and so on. As a result, the airline started an experimental program that placed cabin attendant trainees in the class-room for a certain period and then gave them additional train-ing during an evaluation training flight. On those flights, ex-perienced cabin attendants provided the trainees with struc-tured OJT based on a list of identified job tasks. Some tasks, such as serving meals and snacks, were demonstrated dur-ing the actual delivery of services to passengers. Other tasks were presented to trainees away from passengers during the relatively free periods between meal service.

The coal extraction division of American Electric Power uses structured OJT as part of its broad safety training pro-grams. Safety training conducted in the classroom focuses primarily on the rules and regulations related to safe work practices and the handling of hazardous materials. In the work setting, task trainers train each employee, managers and hourly employees alike, on specific knowledge and skills re-lated to safety in their immediate work area. The results sug-gest that training that addresses different training objectives in different training locations improves safety outcomes. For example, in one coal mine, training significantly reduced the number of lost days caused by back injuries.

Selection Factors

We have seen that organizations can use structured OJT in a variety of ways. The question remains: Under what conditions should we use structured OJT? As we have already stated, structured OJT should be used only when analysis shows that employees are not performing as required because they lack the required knowledge and skills. That is the principal reason for taking such action. Our point is that an informed decision should be made each time structured OJT is considered for use.

We rely on five selection factors when we determine whether structured OJT is appropriate for a given training situation: the nature of the task, the resources available, constraints in the work setting, financial considerations, and individual differences.

In practice, the selection factors should be used in connection with an inventory listing the tasks that employees should learn. Each task on the inventory should be matched with the selection factors to determine whether structured OJT is suitable for it.

Nature of the Task

The first selection factor concerns the nature of the task. Four issues are related to the nature of the task: immediacy, frequency, difficulty, and consequence of error.

Immediacy. Do employees require the task information right now, or can they receive it later on without hurting production or service delivery? Managers often consider immediacy to be the most crucial issue. At times, the best approach may be to dispense information by bringing groups together off the job. Structured OJT can be suitable when logistical or scheduling problems prevent individuals from being brought together as a group.

Frequency. Frequency involves the number of times an employee performs the task during a given work period. Some tasks, such as giving performance feedback to subordinates or maintaining equipment, can be performed only once or twice per year. Other tasks can be performed many times during a single workday. Structured OJT may be easier to schedule when a task is done often.

Difficulty. Task difficulty should be thought of in terms not only of inherent difficulty but also of employees' abilities. Some tasks can be difficult simply because employees lack the prerequisites required to perform the task. Other employees may find them easier. Nevertheless, structured OJT can be suitable for difficult tasks because it makes the information more concrete. Structured OJT may not be suitable for tasks that involve speed of performance or safety hazards. And some low-difficulty tasks can be acquired with the aid of job performance guides alone.

Consequences of Error. The consequences of error in the performance of a task should also be considered. What are the consequences to the organization or to individuals if the task is not performed correctly? The consequences can represent lost customers, reduced profits, destroyed property, psychological harm, or physical injury. Tasks where the consequences of error are high and difficulty is low may be more suitable for structured OJT than tasks where the consequences of error and difficulty are both high. Tasks where difficulty is high can be learned with the aid of simulators or in off-the-job practice areas. These settings allow and can even encourage employees to make errors so that they can view the results of error first-hand without doing permanent harm.

Available Resources
The second selection factor is the resources available in the job setting that can be used in the training. Structured OJT requires trainees to be able to do something or know something at the end of the training session. For such outcomes to be achieved, the various resources required for the training

must be available in the work setting. Three kinds of resources must be considered: people, time for training, and
equipment, tools, or data.

People. People deliver structured OJT, and they are sometimes needed to support it. Above all, structured OJT requires
experienced employees, who conduct the training. The organization may not have employees who are experts in a given
task. This situation often occurs when a new piece of equipment or technology is brought in and no one on site has had
time to develop sufficient expertise. In such cases, selected
employees must either be sent away to an off-site training
program or be given time to develop the expertise that they
need on their own. Then, they can use structured OJT to train
others.

Time for Training. The next crucial question is whether
there is adequate time for training during the workday. Managers are often reluctant to take their best performers away
from the job, even for short periods of time. Managers have
been heard to say: "We are too busy." "We can't stop production to train people in this way." "It sounds nice to have the
OJT structured and all, but it seems better suited for companies that don't have our tight schedules."

Attempting to squeeze both work and structured OJT into
the same work schedule is generally not productive. The quality both of the work and of the training suffers. Whenever
work time and training time have to compete, work usually
wins. In many instances, structured OJT is conducted at times
other than regular work hours, such as before work, during
breaks, or after the workday.

Equipment, Tools, and Data. When structured OJT trains
employees how to use equipment, tools, or data, these resources must be available in the work setting. Making them
available can pose logistical problems. A busy organization

generally cannot take a piece of production equipment out of service just for training purposes. Alternate ways have to be found when work schedules are tight. For instance, Eddie Bauer, Inc., has designated training areas on the warehouse floor at which structured OJT is delivered to newly hired warehouse employees. If the proper equipment, tools, or data cannot be provided in the work setting, then structured OJT is probably not suitable.

Constraints in the Job Setting

To some extent, any job setting is an inconvenient place in which to conduct training, and thus virtually all job settings have constraints. Flexibility and creativity are often required to make sure that training does not become a burden for managers or for employees. Two constraints must always be considered: training location and work distractions.

Training Location. Here are some suitable locations for structured OJT: an office, a training station within the production area, a conference room, a computer station, a work bench, an assembly line, an observation booth, a lunchroom, the passenger cabin of a commercial airliner. As we described earlier, training staff at KLM Royal Dutch Airlines report that structured OJT is being conducted for flight attendants during flights and even in front of passengers. Follow-up has shown that training has no effect on service quality and that passengers generally appreciate seeing the training take place. Structured OJT has even been conducted in an automobile, since this was the most appropriate place for a newly hired cable salesperson to be trained by an experienced salesperson as the two traveled between client locations. The training location selected essentially depends on the training resources necessary to achieve the training objectives.

A number of constraints in the work setting can affect the

suitability of training locations. For instance, structured OJT could not be conducted when both the experienced employee and the trainee were wearing protective bodysuits and oxygen masks in a spray paint booth. In this case, the training was conducted outside the spray paint booth before the gear was put on. It is also inappropriate to conduct structured OJT in circumstances that could embarrass the trainee in front of customers or other employees. If a suitable training location cannot be found, structured OJT is probably not suitable.

Work Distractions. Does the job setting have inherent distractions or performance demands that could inhibit learning, induce stress, or place trainees in physical or psychological jeopardy? Work distractions often include ambient noise, safety hazards, background activity, schedules, or onlookers. When such distractions are conspicuous, they will lessen the effectiveness of any training provided, and they can even lead to unintended violations of safety rules. It is extremely important for training to follow all safety precautions.

In most job settings, there are sufficient distractions to make structured OJT difficult to conduct wihtout taking some preliminary measures. However, only a few environments, such as nuclear power plants or air traffic control towers, are totally inappropriate for training. Learning new job information can be stressful enough in itself, and the additional pressure of relocating during training can take a toll on trainees and trainers alike.

Financial Considerations

Structured OJT has financial considerations that should be taken into account. At the same time, it is wise to view the costs of structured OJT or of any structured training program as an investment from which the organization can expect a return. A decision based on costs alone can be unwise. Two financial elements are important: the number of trainees and the predicted financial benefits.

Number of Trainees. Mangum (1985) has suggested that the suitability of OJT decreases as the number of trainees increases, since the costs associated with off-site training programs can be spread out over more individuals. We agree with this assessment, but we add the following caveat: We distinguish between the total number of people trained and the number of people who need training at any one time. Structured OJT is appropriate when the number of people who need training at a given time is low, even though the total number of people trained overall is high. Off-the-job training approaches make sense only when large numbers of employees need training at one time. The financial forecasting model described in the next section helps to compare these situations.

Predicted Financial Benefits. Logically, an organization would consider the best deal to be the training approach predicted to provide the most financial benefits at the lowest cost. Until recently, information of this nature was perceived to be useful but hard to obtain. Swanson and Gradous (1988) report a method of comparing the financial benefits that can forecast the benefits of various HRD program options. The method proposes that each program option has a performance value and that benefit equals performance value minus cost.

All other things being equal, structured OJT should be selected only if performance value exceeds cost. Our own research shows that the costs of structured OJT are higher than those of unstructured OJT but that the additional costs resulted in greater financial benefits for the organization (Jacobs, Jones, & Neil, 1992). Thus, cost figures alone cannot be used to determine the suitability of OJT. It is more prudent to consider all aspects of the equation. Structured OJT can cost more, say, than a classroom training course, but it may also provide more financial benefits, since it trains employees more efficiently.

Individual Differences

The individual differences among trainees are the last important factor. While people are alike in many ways, they also differ in ways that can affect the success of a training program. The concern here is whether trainees differ in ways that might hinder the effectiveness of structured OJT. Our experiences suggest that structured OJT affects individual trainees in different ways. Some trainees behave as they would in any other training situation. Others become anxious and withdrawn. A few become defensive about their abilities. Two individual differences deserve consideration: trainee prerequisites and trainee preferences.

Trainee Prerequisites. Regardless of the approach used, training is always more effective when trainees possess the prerequisite knowledge, skills, and readiness. Prerequisite knowledge and skills include technical background, comfort with the use of tools and equipment, literacy, and job experience. Trainees must also be ready to learn a new task. That is, they must anticipate learning the task without undue anxiety or resistance. Of course, we all hope that trainees will enter a training session with enthusiasm and interest.

Having the proper prerequisites seems especially critical when we determine whether to use structured OJT. Structured OJT is not appropriate for conveying information that trainees should already have learned or for arousing interest in a topic that trainees find irrelevant. Some of these issues can be addressed by the way in which training is conducted. However, if critical trainee prerequisites are not present, then structured OJT may not be suitable.

Trainee Preferences. Research has shown that some persons learn more than others simply because the instructional approach has been consistent with their preferred style of learning, which are based on personality variables (Cronbach & Snow, 1977). Thus, it is appropriate to consider personality differences when deciding whether to use structured OJT. For example, field-dependent persons—that is, people who have difficulty perceiving simple figures within a complex field— have more difficulty than field-independent persons in identifying the critical features of concepts, and they ask more questions related to the instruction.

While no one has as yet investigated the relationship between structured OJT and trainee preferences, the results of other studies suggest that there is a relation. And we have observed on a number of occasions that some trainees react better to structured OJT than others, no matter what the content or the trainees' ability to learn the task. Preferences for or against the use of structured OJT may be based on reactions to the relative degree of rigidity that it imposes on the instructional condition.

Summary of Selection Factors

Figure 3.1 summarizes the selection factors discussed above that can help you to decide whether to use structured OJT. The figure also provides space for comments regarding each factor.

In practice, some selection factors may be more relevant than others, and some may not apply at all. Moreover, a final decision is often strongly influenced by subjective factors that the checklist does not account for, such as the preferences of management and the organization's commitment to training. Clearly, these factors also should be taken into account.

Figure 3.1. Structured OJT Selection Factors

Task name: _____

Appropriateness of Factor	*Factor*	*Comments*
_____	Nature of the task	_____
	▪ Immediacy	_____
	▪ Frequency	_____
	▪ Difficulty	
	▪ Consequences of error	
_____	Resources available	_____
	▪ People	_____
	▪ Time for training	
	▪ Equipment, tools, data	_____
_____	Constraints in job setting	_____
	▪ Training location	_____
	▪ Work distractions	
		_____
_____	Financial considerations	_____
	▪ Number of trainees	_____
	▪ Predicted financial benefits	
		_____
_____	Individual differences	_____
	▪ Trainee prerequisites	_____
	▪ Trainee preferences	
		_____

Final decision: _____

_____

_____

Thus, professional judgment plays a part in the making of sound selection decisions.

Conclusion

Although structured OJT has been shown to be effective in many different training situations, it is not appropriate in every situation. An informed decision should be made each time it is considered for use. If structured OJT is selected, the next step in the process is to analyze the task.

Analyzing the Tasks
to Be Learned

ONCE THE DECISION to use structured OJT has been made, the next step of the process is to analyze the tasks that should be learned. This chapter examines the following topics:

❐ What is meant by the *task level of jobs*
❐ How to plan the task analysis
❐ Using the task analysis information.

The Task Level of Jobs

Structured OJT is not meant to train employees how to do an entire job, as we have heard more than a few managers and experienced employees mistakenly say. Rather, structured OJT focuses on small components of jobs that are called *tasks*, or small units of job-related information. Many other training approaches share this same emphasis. But, the task is even more important for structured OJT than it is for these other approaches. Most off-the-job training programs address several job tasks or broad topics of information, perhaps to make the time spent away from the job seem worthwhile. In contrast, structured OJT focuses on a strictly limited set of job-related knowledge and skills.

The notion that jobs are composed of tasks is associated with work done on an assembly line. Nevertheless, the task is still central for jobs in the new economy. As the boundaries between jobs have become less distinct, tasks have more often become the unit of focus. Jobs are less isolated from one another today, so that each task is not necessarily a small operation that has limited meaning, but an effort that results in a completed unit of work. Thus, today's jobs are likely to have task diversity and task complexity.

Every job task has two basic components: a set of well-defined behaviors and the performance outcomes that result from the behaviors.

Consider the task of troubleshooting customer service problems, a task found in many organizations that have a strong customer orientation. The task has both a behavioral component—troubleshooting the customer's problem—and an outcome component—the result must meet the organization's specifications for interacting with customers.

Task Behaviors

Task behaviors are the thoughts, actions, and decisions that one must make in order to do the task. Behaviors are often the most detailed level of analysis used to describe jobs. Since tasks can differ widely in content, we analyze them into different types of behaviors. For example, the task of installing a replacement part on a piece of equipment requires the employee to perform a series of steps in a specified order. The task of identifying the faulty part involves a completely different set of behaviors: matching the symptoms of the problem with its likely causes and then taking the actions required to resolve the problem. While the two tasks—

troubleshooting the problem and installing the replacement part—are highly interdependent, we are justified in considering them to be distinct because each task places differing behavioral demands on the person who performs it.

While task behaviors differ, they tend to differ in fairly consistent patterns. Regardless of job level, most jobs have tasks that require problems to be solved, tasks that require decisions to be made, tasks that require inspections to be done, tasks that require a set of sequential steps to be performed, and so on. Table 4.1 describes eight characteristic sets of behavioral patterns that one commonly finds when analyzing tasks. Some tasks can contain more than one behavioral pattern, as when performing a procedure requires a decision to be made or a problem to be solved.

The behavioral patterns associated with particular tasks tend to be related to type of job. For example, management and supervisory jobs are likely to have tasks involving the behaviors of planning and organizing resources that affect others, while skilled technical jobs are likely to have tasks involving behaviors that make use of tools or objects. We make this generalization mindful of the fact that today's expanded work expectations have created many exceptions to the rule. That is, many managers use tools as part of their jobs, while many skilled technical employees are involved in the planning and organizing of work. Nevertheless, the ability to see and anticipate discrete patterns of work behaviors within tasks, regardless of the job involved, is an important aspect of understanding the task level.

Performance Outcomes

Tasks also have performance outcomes. Performance outcomes describe the results to which the behaviors lead. Performance outcomes can be stated in terms of the *quantity* of products produced or services rendered, the *quality* of

Table 4.1. Patterns of Task Behavior

Behavior	Description	Information to Document
Procedure	Performing a series of steps in a specific order	▪ Steps of the procedure ▪ Quality requirements ▪ Safety information ▪ Embedded decisions and troubleshooting components
Troubleshooting	Matching existing problem situations or symptoms with probable causes and the actions that are likely to resolve them	▪ Possible problems ▪ Probable causes of each problem ▪ Actions to take for each cause
Decision Making	Determining the action to take based on the arrangement of varying conditions in a given situation	▪ Conditions that vary ▪ Decisions related to each set of conditions
Inspecting	Determining the accuracy of the match between a given product or process and a desired model	▪ Inspection areas ▪ Steps in conducting an inspection ▪ Criteria overall and for each area ▪ Examples
Adjusting/ Revising	Changing a product or process in order to meet a standard	▪ Areas to adjust or revise ▪ Effects of making adjustments or revisions ▪ Steps in making the adjustments ▪ Examples
Calculating	Determining the value of separate sets of measures	▪ Steps in the calculation ▪ Consequence of each step ▪ Meaning of the calculation ▪ Examples
Planning	Gathering information and performing or assigning actions to achieve goals	▪ Information to gather ▪ Resources to use ▪ Process steps ▪ Goals to achieve
Comprehending	Recognizing an instance of a class of ideas, actions, or things	▪ Operational definition ▪ Critical attributes ▪ Variable attributes ▪ Positive and negative examples

the products or services provided, the *timeliness* with which they are delivered, and the *costs* of producing the products or services.

Performance outcomes help to determine the adequacy of task behaviors. If the desired performance outcomes are not attained, then the cause may lie in the behaviors of the persons performing the task. We cannot judge the adequacy of the task behaviors without first examining the performance outcomes that result from those behaviors. This is the essence of the performance analysis process.

We use task statements to capture the information that we have about task behaviors and performance outcomes. In structured OJT, we use task statements to communicate the training content and outcomes to trainers and trainees. Task statements help us to clarify the boundaries of tasks. A task statement has two elements: an action verb and an object noun. The action verb describes what the person does, and the object noun describes what the person acts upon or what his or her action affects. We recommend that a task statement contain a single action verb. Here are some typical task statements from a variety of professional, skilled technical, and management and supervisory positions:

- ❏ Calculate interest and principal payments on consumer mortgage loans
- ❏ Troubleshoot customer service problems
- ❏ Determine insurance deductibles based on customer needs
- ❏ Install replacement dies in a metal-stamping machine
- ❏ Present a rationale for financial planning to individuals who request retirement information
- ❏ Facilitate root-cause analysis team meetings.

Each of these task statements represents a distinct set of behaviors and distinct performance outcomes. Most jobs are made up of many tasks. The ability of an experienced employee to perform a task depends on his or her understanding of and ability to carry out the behaviors that make up the task. For someone else to be able to learn the same behaviors and achieve the same outcomes in the most efficient and effective way possible, we must identify the component parts and then organize them in ways that facilitate learning. That is the basic purpose of task analysis.

Planning Task Analysis for Structured OJT

Task analysis is the process of making explicit the behaviors, performance outcomes, prerequisite knowledge, skills, attitudes, and other information relevant to a job task. We use this information to prepare the structured OJT module that corresponds to the task. Because task analysis provides such a wealth of information, it is one of the most critical steps of the process.

Task analysis seeks to find the best way of performing a task while recognizing that *best* is a relative notion. In practice, disagreement can arise over how a task is presently done. We also recognize that the task will change as improvements are made. We use task analysis to capture what is best for the organization at a particular moment. In this sense, task analysis seeks to show those who must perform a task how to complete it without risk of physical or psychological harm, in the shortest time and with the least effort, and at the lowest cost.

Task analysis is usually conducted as an iterative activity in which task information is gathered and draft documents are prepared, are reviewed by experts and stakeholders, and revised as their comments suggest. Often, the cycle just described is repeated several times before the analysis is complete.

You can plan a task analysis for structured OJT by constructing a matrix that matches information sources with data-gathering methods for each of the major products covered by the task analysis. For example, Figure 4.1 presents the plan for analyzing our sample task, troubleshooting customer service problems. Under the plan shown in Figure 4.1, we will observe and interview experienced employees in order to gather information about task behaviors. We will gather information about performance outcomes by reviewing performance appraisal documents and by interviewing experienced employees and supervisors. We will obtain information about customer requirements and quality by reviewing existing training materials, reviewing company standards, and interviewing experts.

As Figure 4.1 suggests, each product covered by the task analysis may require a different source of information and a different method of gathering the information. Your selection of sources and methods should be based on the purpose of the analysis, the nature of the task information, the accessibility of experts, and time constraints and other organizational factors. Several works can help you to match sources and methods: Swanson (1994), Jonassen, Hannum, and Tessmer (1989), Carlisle (1986), and Zemke and Kramlinger (1984) are all useful. Most authorities recommend that you use as many different sources and methods as possible, since it helps to reduce the kind of systematic error that can result from the use of any one source or method alone.

Products of Task Analysis

A task analysis typically has four major products: task behaviors, performance outcomes, prerequisites, and resources and additional information about safety and quality.

Task Behaviors. The goal of task analysis is to identify the exact nature of the behaviors required to do a task. In identifying them, it also identifies the relationships between them. For example, for a procedural task, it determines which

Figure 4.1. Task Analysis Plan

Task name: Troubleshooting Customer Service Problems			
Information Sources/Data-Gathering Methods			
Products	Analyze existing task analysis reports, standard operating procedures, training manuals, customer requirements, internal quality standards, and safety information	Observe experts as they perform the task	Interview experts about the task	Ask experts to respond to question-naires about the task
Task Behaviors		X	X	
Performance Outcomes	X		X	
Prerequisites	X		X	
Resources	X	X		
Safety/ Quality Information	X		X	

step comes first, which comes second, and so on. When we view all the behaviors together, we can see the underlying pattern: procedure, decision making, problem solving, inspection, concept, or principle, among others. These behaviors form the content of the structured OJT program.

Performance Outcomes. Task analysis also seeks to make explicit the performance outcomes that result from the behaviors. As we have already noted, performance outcomes can be stated in terms of the quantity, quality, and cost of the products or services that result from performance of the task.

Prerequisites. In the process of analyzing the task behaviors, we identify the prerequisite areas of knowledge, skills, and attitudes. Successful performance of a task requires the employees who perform it to possess the necessary prerequisites.

Resources. Task analysis also identifies the resources required to do a task. These resources can include specialized tools, equipment, data, people, and time. Listing these resources can also reveal more general areas of prerequisite knowledge and skills, such as basic knowledge of tool usage, math and reading skills, computer literacy, or blueprint reading, to name only a few.

Additional Task Information. Additional task information can include quality requirements, safety precautions, or special hazards or difficulty—any information pertaining to the task that might be useful when we prepare the structured OJT module.

Information Sources

The sources of information for a task analysis can basically be separated into two major categories: documents and people.

Documents. Organizations typically have an array of documents that describe how a task has been done in the past and how it should be done in the future. These documents can include previous task analysis reports, standard operating procedures, manufacturer's manuals, technical manuals, customer information, and safety specifications. Documents are especially useful when the task represents a totally new area of expertise in the organization, as it does when new technology is introduced, and when the number of experienced employees is small.

People. The people who can provide the information required for task analysis can include experienced employees, job incumbents, supervisors, safety specialists, engineers, union officials, and representatives from external suppliers.

Gathering information from these individuals can sometimes be difficult, simply because of the nature of experts. Beyond possessing more skill than their peers in some specific domain, experts have unique ways of thinking and using information that differ sharply from those of most others around them (Chi, Glaser, & Farr, 1988).

These differences sometimes make it difficult for them to communicate task information. Our work with experts leads to the following observations:

❐ Experts always seem to demonstrate or explain their work behaviors quickly and with a great deal of ease.

❐ Experts have rarely given much thought to their actions before you ask them about them, and their work behaviors have in many instances become automatic.

❐ Experts usually believe that most of what they do is easy, and they cannot understand why others have difficulty attaining the same level of expertise.

❐ Several experts who perform the same task usually each have their own way of doing the task, although the essential aspects of how each performs the task is similar in most respects, and the performance outcomes are the same as well.

❐ Experts often say one thing and do another, primarily because they are not totally aware of all the things they do.

Thus, in order to gather accurate and complete information, we need to observe experienced employees carefully to make certain that what they say and do are consistent.

Information-Gathering Methods

There are four methods of gathering task analysis information: observation, interviews, questionnaires, and content analysis.

Observation. Observation helps to make even the most subtle work behaviors explicit. Experts do not always realize that they are doing something, and thus they do not report it. Observation helps us to fill the gaps that result.

Interviews. Talking to experts in different venues is another way of gathering task information. Formal interviews can be conducted individually, in small groups, or as part of group process activities, which can include the use of a focus group or nominal group technique.

Questionnaires. Giving experts a task inventory and asking them to react is probably the most often used way of gathering task information. Questionnaires allow large numbers of people to supply information about specific aspects of the task, such as task difficulty, task frequency, and training requirements.

Content Analysis. Synthesizing the information culled from documents and other printed resources into outlines, graphs, and tables is another method of gathering task information.

To summarize, considering the sources and the methods appropriate for each product of the task analysis helps us to plan a task analysis before we begin. But one must never view a plan as unalterable. Unanticipated issues and constraints can often arise. For instance, particular experienced employees can be called away from their jobs. In such cases, you will have to rely on other people for information—perhaps also on documents.

Using the Task Analysis Information

Once you have completed the task analysis, you need to make the information useful for the preparation of structured OJT modules. This usually involves three basic activities: specifying training objectives, organizing task behaviors for learning purposes, and developing performance tests to accompany the training.

Specify Training Objectives

Training objectives are statements that describe the behavior expected of the trainee at the conclusion of structured OJT. Training objectives are derived from performance outcomes, which are identified as part of the task analysis. According to Mager (1984), training objectives have three components: the *conditions* under which the trainee demonstrates his or her ability to do the task, including such things as the use of resources, constraints, and setting; the *behaviors* that the trainee must demonstrate when performing the task; and the *standards* by which the learned behavior is judged—time, accuracy, or quantity.

In most instances, the standards component of training objectives necessarily differs from the levels expected by performance outcomes. Performance outcomes describe expectations when experienced employees perform the task. Trainees are not likely to achieve these levels when they begin to learn the task. Thus, the standards component of training objectives should accommodate the abilities of trainees who do not have the benefit of experience or prolonged practice.

Organize Task Behaviors

Task behaviors must be organized in a way that makes them easy to learn. Often, this means representing the task in a way that seems totally different from the way in which the task is actually accomplished. Consider that the way in which conceptual information is organized can bear little resemblance to the way in which the information is used on the job. Describing an operational definition, specifying critical and variable attributes, and developing positive and negative examples are all part of analyzing conceptual information.

The hierarchical analysis technique (Gagne, Briggs, & Wager, 1988) can be used to organize related sets of conceptual information.

Some other task behaviors, such as problem solving and decision making, may appear to be linear activities. In fact, when we organize problem-solving behaviors, the result usually looks like a table of information that matches problem situations with causes and actions. Decision-making behaviors are usually organized by matching varying conditions with different actions. In cases like these, we may have to do some additional work in order to facilitate the learning of task behaviors by others.

At this point, we should include any additional task information that was generated by task analysis. As we have already noted, the additional task information can include such issues as safety and quality. Often, the additional task information can be represented in the form of visuals, such as photographs, illustrations, or drawings.

Develop Performance Tests

Performance tests can also be developed at this time. As we note later, most structured OJT makes use of tests that measure a trainee's ability to do something, not just to know something. For that reason, most tests that accompany structured OJT take the form of performance-rating scales.

The trainer uses performance-rating scales at the end of training to assess either the completed product that results from the trainee's efforts or the process that the trainee used to achieve the product. You use *product measures* for evaluating end products, and you use *process measures* for evaluating how the end product was achieved. For example, judging the adequacy of a sales plan calls for a product scale, while judging the planning behaviors that went into the sales plan calls for a process scale. Additional information about

Figure 4.2. Task Analysis Summary Sheet

Task name: _____

A. Data-gathering methods   _____

                                                    _____

                                                    _____

B. Information sources   _____

                                                    _____

                                                    _____

C. Training objective

    ▪ Performance condition   _____

    ▪ Task behavior   _____

    ▪ Standard   Time: _____
        behaviors

                                          Accuracy: _____

                                          Quantity: _____

D. Ways of organizing task   _____
       behaviors

                                                    _____

                                                    _____

E. Type of performance test   _____

                                                    _____

                                                    _____

developing different types of performance tests can be obtained from Shrock and Coscarelli (1989) and from Westgaard (1993).

Figure 4.2 presents a summary sheet that helps to ensure that a task analysis has been planned adequately and that the resulting task analysis information is ready for use in preparing the structured OJT module. Chapter Six describes the preparation of structured OJT modules.

Conclusion

Once the decision has been made to use structured OJT, the tasks to be learned must be analyzed in depth. Structured OJT focuses on the task level or on small sets of job information. Tasks represent small units of behavior and their performance outcomes. Task analysis is the process of identifying the component parts of tasks and gathering relevant information about them. The resulting task analysis information is used to prepare the structured OJT modules.

CHAPTER 5

Selecting, Training, and Managing Employees to Deliver Structured OJT

THE QUESTION OF who should deliver structured OJT tends to arise early in the process. Should the delivery of structured OJT be limited to certain employees only, such as supervisors and selected frontline employees? Or should all experienced employees be expected to conduct structured OJT? These questions should be addressed before the organization uses structured OJT. This chapter answers two questions:

❐ What are the basic requirements for structured OJT trainers?
❐ How do you select, train, and manage structured OJT trainers?

Basic Trainer Requirements

In its most basic form, structured OJT involves having an experienced employee or trainer present job-related information to another employee one-on-one. However, structured OJT means more than just having Sam teach Joe how to do his job (Kondrasuk, 1979). Structured OJT trainers have basic requirements in two areas: They must have adequate knowledge and skills in the task, and they must have adequate knowledge, skills, and attitudes as a trainer.

If trainers do not meet the requirements in both areas, the effectiveness and efficiency of the training are likely to be at risk. However well the other steps of the structured OJT process have been performed, much of the success of structured OJT—or of any training program, for that matter—depends on the trainer's having the right skills (Powers, 1992). Our view does not mean that the number of employees whom you can involve as trainers is limited. Indeed, we believe that many more employees than you may have believed can be involved as structured OJT trainers. The issue is one of using the right employees in each situation.

Selecting and Training Trainers

Traditionally, those who have delivered OJT have been supervisors or certain frontline employees, such as leadpersons, who are recognized as experts. This expectation continues in many organizations today (Broadwell, 1986). Yet in reality, few trainers ever receive sufficient preparation, although this situation has begun to change. Increasing numbers of companies are recognizing that they must select and train their OJT trainers in a comprehensive and formal way.

Nevertheless, in most instances, few trainers receive more than a single program on coaching or one-on-one training techniques. This isolated training experience is rarely enough to ensure that the training provided will be reliable (Wichman, 1989). At best, existing programs offer an overview of one small part of the process—delivering the content. At worst, they mislead managers into believing that such experience is all that trainer development requires.

Selecting and training experienced employees to be structured OJT trainers, whether they are managers, supervisors, or experienced frontline employees, is a process in itself. The process has four steps: (1) identify selection criteria, (2) select trainers, (3) train trainers, and (4) manage trainer performance.

Identify Selection Criteria

Each task imposes its own set of trainer selection criteria. Nevertheless, we believe that every structured OJT trainer requires some measure of the qualities described below:

☐ *Task knowledge and skills.* Task knowledge and skills involve the documented ability to perform the work behaviors and achieve the performance outcomes at a level that consistently meets or exceeds expectations.

☐ *Specialized training.* The completion of specialized training or education programs can be an important requirement. Such training may represent new areas of expertise for the trainer's organization.

☐ *Willingness to share.* Trainers should have a temperament that enables them to share their experiences and expertise with others. They should be interested in the development of other employees.

☐ *Respect from peers.* Many trainers are already perceived by other employees as having special status as the result of task expertise, leadership abilities, general problem-solving skills, or knowledge of the organization.

☐ *Interpersonal skills.* Interpersonal skills involve the individual's ability to express complex ideas clearly and comprehensively during everyday interactions.

☐ *Literacy skills.* Every trainer must be able to comprehend resource materials or perform calculations related to the task.

❏ *Concern for the organization.* Trainers should show an interest in helping the organization to improve its performance. They can demonstrate such an interest by participating in continuous improvement efforts, following safe work practices, and doing things that help the organization to achieve its goals.

❏ *Job expectations.* Some experienced employees have job expectations or assignments that might affect their ability to perform as a trainer.

The importance of the criteria just reviewed is likely to differ with the task. While task knowledge and skills can be the most important criteria to consider for some tasks, they are not necessarily the most important criteria for all tasks. For example, tasks involving highly technical information logically require the selection process to emphasize the employees who possess task knowledge, possibly at the expense of other criteria. But tasks that contain more general information, as they do when the training content describes a work process, may require trainers to have less task knowledge than other criteria, such as concern for the organization. Ultimately, management in cooperation with supervisors and job incumbents should determine the best mix of criteria for a given task.

Select Trainers

Typically, the employees who have held a job the longest or who have the highest status in their work group are the ones who are asked to be trainers. However, reliance on the criteria reviewed in the preceding section has the effect of involving more employees in the training and of bringing a wider variety of individuals into the training process. In this sense, the selection criteria that we advocate can involve employees who in the past have not had an opportunity to be trainers.

Once you have settled on the selection criteria, you can select prospective structured OJT trainers from one or the other of two basic groups of employees: *staff trainers* who are already adept at the training process, such as members of HRD staff, and who should acquire expertise in the task and *experienced employees,* including supervisors and frontline employees, who should attain expertise in the training process.

It is impossible to say that one group is better in all instances, because much depends on factors within the organization and on the nature of the task. Those who favor using only staff trainers make the point that this practice limits work disruptions, because line employees do not have to drop what they are doing in order to conduct training. They add that work locations can vary and that it is easier to send staff trainers to the trainee's location than it is to bring trainees to trainers. Many organizations now use itinerant structured OJT trainers. Finally, reliance on staff trainers minimizes the risk of violating contractual agreements that prevent employees from undertaking training responsibilities.

While these are compelling reasons, it is not always appropriate to use staff trainers. We have noticed a general movement toward having experienced employees become trainers. One major advantage of this approach is that these individuals possess in-depth knowledge of the task. Needless to say, staff trainers cannot be expected to be proficient in every task in an organization or work area for which training is required. Moreover, even when staff trainers do have task expertise, the depth of their knowledge is likely to decline, because only those who perform the task continuously can know all its ins and outs.

Another advantage of using experienced employees as trainers is that the practice spreads the training responsibility out among employees. The ideal of a learning organization re-mains only an ideal unless as many individuals as possible be-come actively involved in sharing their expertise with others. One critical factor in the drive to achieve training objectives is the trainee's receptiveness to learning the knowledge and skills. Often, trainees are more willing to accept information from people who actually perform the task and who can pro-vide additional guidance as needed.

While we generally prefer to use experienced employees as trainers, we are aware that sometimes staff trainers should be used. Moreover, we recognize that not every experienced employee is capable of becoming a trainer. That is, many ex-perienced employees are simply not interested in becoming involved in any way, or their superiors may deem their tal-ents better used elsewhere in the organization. Still others may want to become a trainer but fail to meet certain selec-tion criteria (Leach, 1991).

Once the selection criteria have been identified, the se-lection of trainers can proceed in any one of a variety of ways:

❑   *General announcement.* An announcement can be made throughout the organization encouraging interested employ-ees to sign up for consideration. Managers and human re-sources staff can apply the selection criteria selected by the organization to the individuals who respond to this call. This approach can attract a fairly wide cadre of qualified train-ers who represent both line and staff areas.

❑   *Nomination.* Supervisors and managers can nominate cer-tain individuals who have expertise in the tasks that have been identified for structured OJT. Some of these individu-als may already be known if they served as subject matter experts during the task analysis.

❐ *Recruiting*. Line managers, first-line supervisors, or advanced-level frontline employees may be actively recruited as structured OJT trainers. Furthermore, the selection criteria for being a structured OJT trainer may be used when considering whether to promote or develop certain employees.

Whichever of these approaches is selected, the usual next step is to interview candidates or have them participate in simulations. For example, prospective structured OJT trainers can be asked to demonstrate a simple procedure, such as assembling a flashlight. Their performance can be rated according to some criteria, such as their comfort in speaking in front of others. The final selection decisions can be based on the resulting information.

The last issue related to the selection of trainers that we will review here concerns the matching of trainers and trainees. Such matching is commonly based on some variable of importance, such as the individuals' respective backgrounds, styles, or attitudes. While this issue can affect the success of training, we believe that care taken in regard to other parts of the system can make up for many of these differences. Research from a number of different perspectives has assessed the effects of matches or mismatches between individuals in social situations. Matching has not conclusively been shown to improve outcomes. While it seems evident that individuals can sense when they share something with those around them, they often cannot articulate the precise nature of their commonalities.

In practice, the selection of individuals to serve as structured OJT trainers often faces more constraints than the preceding discussion suggests. No more than one or two individuals may have expertise in a given task. Or there may be constraints on who is actually available. No matter what the constraints, it is important to both the organization and to the employees selected that specific criteria be used to select the structured OJT trainers.

Train Trainers

Once the trainers have been selected, they need to undergo a focused training and development program that will give them the knowledge and skills that they need to deliver structured OJT. Most organizations eventually design their own programs, primarily because the commercially available programs lack the necessary depth, relevance, and fit with the other parts of the organization's structured OJT effort.

Any program used to train structured OJT trainers should enable trainees to:

❒ State the features of structured OJT.
❒ Predict the organizational consequences of using structured and unstructured OJT.
❒ Demonstrate how to analyze tasks in which they have expertise (optional).
❒ Demonstrate how to prepare various components of structured OJT modules (optional).
❒ Demonstrate how to get ready for delivering structured OJT.
❒ Demonstrate the ability to deliver structured OJT by making use of the appropriate instructional events.
❒ Apply criteria to evaluate the effectiveness of their own training (Jacobs, 1990).

If no relevant modules are available for use in the trainer training program, the organization may ask trainees to help develop the modules as part of the program itself. While this expectation may seem to place an undue burden on them, it does have at least two advantages. First, having a meaningful context may well help experienced employees to become more effective trainers. Second, experienced employees often have greater feelings of ownership if they participate in the development of the training.

The amount of time required to achieve these objectives is usually twelve hours of group-based training making use of printed workbooks, videotaped examples of case studies, and various small-group activities. At the conclusion of the in-class experience, each trainee delivers at least one of the structured OJT modules that he or she will be expected to deliver on the job.

People often ask whether structured OJT is appropriate for training structured OJT trainers. The answer is that it can be appropriate when only one or two individuals require such training but that it is usually better to train trainers in a classroom setting. Such a setting makes it possible for trainees to receive feedback from peers and to discuss the organizational ramifications of using structured OJT.

In some organizations, the development experience is not considered to be complete until the trainee is observed delivering a module in the actual job setting. Only after successfully completing all the activities is the employee qualified to deliver structured OJT. Some organizations formalize successful completion by awarding a certificate of accomplishment.

Manage Trainer Performance

Once a group of experienced employees qualified as trainers has been constituted, the organization needs to consider how to maintain and improve their performance over time. Any discussion of these issues should first acknowledge that different individuals have different motives for becoming a trainer. Some people seek to become a trainer for strictly personal reasons, such as the opportunity to gain the respect of others. Others may be motivated by organizational incentives, such as opportunities for development, status, recognition, pay, or promotability. The organization's managers and employee representatives should decide what consequences are appropriate.

Our experience suggests the following points about maintaining and improving trainer performance: First, while individuals may have different motives for becoming a trainer, the organization should take specific actions to maintain the strength of those motives over time. Becoming a trainer involves the expense of additional time and effort, which may not be apparent to some employees at first. The initial interest can be dampened by the unexpected amount of work involved in becoming a trainer.

Second, although the use of financial incentives can be appropriate in certain circumstances, as when becoming a trainer also involves an upgrade in role or promotion, it is in general terms to be discouraged. For one thing, some positions may actually require the incumbent to act as a trainer. Additional compensation is not appropriate in such cases. Second, financial rewards can needlessly complicate the situation, since giving differential pay to employees can involve contractual or personnel issues. Moreover, it is likely that the same trainer performance can be achieved through offerings that are not financial in nature.

Third, certain low key recognition techniques and regularly scheduled opportunities for professional development usually satisfy the needs of most employees. We have seen organizations use a number of nonfinancial rewards with success:

❐ Specially printed coffee cups, pins, or caps denoting that the person is a qualified trainer

☐ Certificates that can be hung in an office or work area

☐ Follow-up meetings that give trainers an opportunity to discuss the various individual issues and concerns that they may have as a result of conducting the training

☐ Meetings at which trainers and managers can discuss ways of improving the use of structured OJT

☐ Permission to attend professional meetings and conferences off-site that focus on OJT and other related topics

☐ Periodic feedback sessions based on observations of trainers during delivery of structured OJT.

All the nonfinancial incentives just enumerated are designed to maintain and improve trainer performance. At the very least, becoming a structured OJT trainer should not place an undue burden on the employee. That would defeat the purpose of the entire effort. To prevent the trainer role from becoming a burden, management should be prepared to provide the resources required to cover trainers when they participate in training activities outside their own work area.

The summary sheet in Figure 5.1 is designed to guide the trainer development process. Because the effectiveness of structured OJT depends so strongly on the quality of trainers, the trainer development process should involve as many groups as possible, including management, staff, and appropriate employee representatives.

Conclusion

In structured OJT, experienced employees present important job knowledge and skills to other persons. That is why it is important to develop experienced employees as trainers. This chapter has presented a four-step process that addresses the development of structured OJT trainers. To a large extent, the

Figure 5.1. Structured OJT Trainer Development Summary Sheet

Task name: _____

A. Identify selection criteria *(check those that apply)*

    1. Task knowledge and skills _____

    2. Specialized training _____

    3. Willingness to share _____

    4. Respect of peers _____

    5. Interpersonal skills _____

    6. Literacy skills _____

    7. Concern for the organization _____

    8. Job expectations _____

B. Select the trainers *(identify groups who will train)*

    1. Staff trainers _____

    2. Line managers _____

    3. Line employees _____

C. Train the trainers *(select objectives of the training)*

    1. Understand structured OJT _____

    2. Understand unstructured OJT _____

    3. Conduct task analysis _____

    4. Prepare structured OJT modules _____

    5. Deliver structured OJT _____

    6. Evaluate trainer effectiveness _____

D. Manage trainer performance *(incentives for trainers)*

    1. Coffee cups, pins, caps, etc. _____

    2. Meetings among trainers _____

    3. Professional meetings off-site _____

    4. Direct observations of trainers _____

effectiveness of structured OJT depends on involving the best employees as trainers. *Best* depends on the criteria selected for trainers in a given task. Using frontline employees close to the task improves the transfer of expertise within the organization, and it gives the organization an opportunity to provide job enrichment for deserving employees.

C H A P T E R 6

Preparing the Training Modules

STRUCTURED OJT IS superior to most other forms of training that occur in the job setting chiefly because it is structured. Structure helps it to achieve the desired training objectives more efficiently and effectively each time it is used. The training modules used in structured OJT contribute much to its success. The following topics are discussed in this chapter:

❑ The components and formats of structured OJT modules
❑ Three types of training
❑ The preparation of structured OJT modules.

Structured OJT Modules

We call the sets of printed instructional materials that accompany structured OJT programs *modules*. A structured OJT module is an organized package that contains all the information necessary to deliver training. Like a lesson plan, a structured OJT module documents the training content and addresses the delivery of training. However, since structured

OJT can be delivered by a variety of individuals, the typical structured OJT module is both more comprehensive and more self-contained than a traditional lesson plan.

In practice, structured OJT modules are the documents that trainers and trainees have in hand during the training process. As we explain in Chapters Seven and Eight, trainers use the modules as they get ready to deliver the training, as reference when they deliver the training, and as they rate the performance of trainees after training. Trainees receive a slightly modified version of the modules so that they can preview the training content and objectives before training, follow the instructor during training, and review what they are expected to perform after the training. When structured OJT modules are used in these ways, they play an important role in ensuring the success of training.

Module Components

Most structured OJT modules include the basic components described below.

Title. The title presents the content of the module in explicit terms. To promote consistency and clarity, we recommend taking the module title verbatim from the task statement or the information on which training content is based.

Rationale Statement. The rationale statement tells the trainee why the training is important by stating what the trainee can do with the knowledge and skills that he or she acquires in the training. The rationale statement should also focus on the importance of the information to the development of individual employees or the organization's effort to attain long-term goals.

Training Objectives. The training objectives specify what the trainee should know or be able to do as a result of the training. As we explained in Chapter Four, training objectives should be referenced to job expectations. In preparing the module, you may find it useful to state the training objective in terms familiar to the targeted trainees, such as by using a "statement of purpose" instead of a "training objective." Both the trainer and the trainee should clearly understand the meaning of the training objectives.

Trainee Prerequisites. Trainee prerequisites are the knowledge, skills, and attitudes that trainees must possess on entering the training session. Trainees have obtained this information from previous training programs or from work experiences. Trainers use these prerequisites to determine the readiness of trainees for training. It also helps trainees to determine their own readiness for training.

Training Resources. Since training occurs in the job setting, trainers should gather together any data, equipment, tools, and instructional materials that training calls for. The scheduling of structured OJT often depends on the availability of resources. Resources used in ongoing work of the organization will have to be taken off-line so that training can be conducted. Specifying the resources needed for training in the training module itself helps to limit interruptions in training while a trainer looks for, say, a document or a tool.

Training Content. The training module should document the training completely. The training content can be presented in a variety of ways, depending on the nature of the task. Training guides (or job performance aids) are extremely useful for procedural, troubleshooting, and decision-making tasks—indeed, for any task that requires a trainee to learn how to apply a technical skill or conceptual information (Rossett & Gautier-Downes, 1991). Tasks involving concepts or principles may require instead that training content be represented in structured text format (Jonassen, 1982).

In most cases, it is preferable for a module to combine training guides with structured text materials. We encourage flexibility in the presentation of training content.

Training Events. How should training be delivered? This is the question that trainers most often ask—understandably, for them it is the most visible part of structured OJT. Training events describe how to deliver structured OJT to trainees in the most effective way. As we describe in Chapter Seven, delivery of structured OJT typically involves five training events: prepare the trainee, present the training, require a response, provide feedback, and evaluate performance.

Performance Tests and Feedback Forms. At the conclusion of training, the trainer should certify that a trainee has successfully achieved the training objective. Thus, most modules include performance tests, such as performance-rating scales or cognitive tests. A module can also contain forms that document the completion of training and provide summative feedback certifying that the training objectives have been achieved.

Organizations use this information in different ways. Some organizations purposely integrate this information into the employee's development plan and require that the information be maintained in a formal way. Other organizations use the forms only for employee feedback. However, an increasing number of organizations use the feedback forms for personnel planning and employee development. In these organizations, when a trainee completes training, copies of the completed forms are sent to the employee's supervisor or to human resource staff so that the employee's development record can be updated. How the rating forms are used often depends on the nature of the job, the requirements of customers, or the potential consequences of error when the task is performed. Figure 6.1 shows a training schedule that one organization uses to document the completion of structured OJT modules. Completed training schedules become part of the trainee's development plan.

Figure 6.1. Sample Training Schedule

TRAINING SCHEDULE			
Prepared for:		Date:	
Prepared by:		Revised:	
Module	Date Started	Date Finished	Trainer
a. Conducting a performance appraisal session			
b. Resolving conflicts between employees			
c. Scheduling customer orders			
d. Conducting a team meeting			

An increasing number of organizations require employees to become certified in the performance of tasks that are critical to the achievement of outcomes. Many of these organizations certify employees to comply with the ISO 9000 quality standards. One effective way of meeting customer requirements is to use performance tests with structured OJT.

Additional Information. A training module can also include additional information that serves to supplement or enrich the training content. This additional information can include such things as internal technical documents, blueprints, customer satisfaction data, safety manuals, technical documents, or reprints from professional magazines and journals.

Module Formats

Once the training module's components have been prepared, the next step is to determine the format in which they should be assembled. We have used five different formats: short form, spiral-bound booklet, three-ring binder, printed booklet with permanent binding, and embedded text.

Short Form. The simplest and most expedient format for a structured OJT module is the short form, which consists of just one or very few pages. Modules in this format can be prepared in relatively little time, and the cost is low. This format seems especially suited when the task is relatively short in length or it has few complications, when resources are limited, or when the task or the information presented is expected to change soon. Laminated card stock is often used for the pages.

For one organization alone we have prepared more than twenty short form modules. These modules are stored in a metal book rack in the work setting. The location makes the modules easily accessible. Each module is available in two versions. Trainers use a laminated version as reference during training and put it back on the rack when the training is completed. Trainees receive a nonlaminated giveaway version before training. They are instructed to review the information before training and to refer to it during training. Many employees keep the module after training for reference.

While we have had much success with this format, we caution against its overuse. The short form is effective for many situations, but not for all. It is always a challenge to maintain the details and complexity of training content while presenting them in a way that makes the information accessible and useful. The short form can tempt one to oversimplify the training content, and oversimplication runs the risk of omitting critical information. A thorough analysis of the task is still a prerequisite when the short form is used.

Spiral-Bound Booklet. One step up from the short form is the spiral-bound booklet. The spiral binding is located lengthwise on a full sheet of standard-size paper or on the short side of standard paper cut in half. Both cover and pages are most often made of stiff card stock. This format seems especially suited when the training content involves complex actions, lengthy procedures, or complex troubleshooting. Line drawings or photographs can be added as necessary.

The spiral-bound booklet is more permanent than the short form. Its usefulness may be limited for some training content, such as detailed text information. The horizontal aspect ratio enables the spiral-bound booklet to be propped up at the workstation, and the worker has both hands free to perform the task. The spiral-bound booklet seems best suited to situations in which the trainee and the trainer can use the module from a distance.

Three-Ring Binder. The three-ring binder format makes it possible to present structured text information along with a variety of accompanying resources. For example, in addition to text information, a three-ring binder can easily hold folded blueprints, schematics, or other large reference materials. It can also accommodate an appendix section for enrichment materials that could be shared with trainees after training. Finally, a binder can include zippered pockets holding small tools, such as slide rules and micrometers, and other materials that are part of the training content.

These additional resources are usually considered to be dedicated parts of the module. They should not be removed for other purposes. Having the training resources readily available in the module allows flexibility and creativity when the trainer presents the training, when the trainee practices and responds to the training, and when the trainer evaluates the trainee's performance. A self-contained module facilitates all these activities. The three-ring binder format has two possible disadvantages: the cost of the binders and the resources that go into the binders.

Printed Booklet with Permanent Binding. If the training content is unlikely to change and if many individuals will require training, then a printed booklet with permanent binding can be the most appropriate format. This format can present several different varieties of training content. However, the permanent binding limits its flexibility. Nonetheless, modules in this format can be produced at relatively low cost when large numbers of copies are required.

Embedded Text. Finally, if the structured OJT involves the use of computers, it is sometimes possible to present the training content as embedded text. Embedded text can be used in conjunction with internal menu prompts or off-the-shelf computer shells that can be purchased to accompany many commercially produced software programs. In most cases, modules in this format are used in conjunction with materials in some other format, such as spiral-bound booklet or short form.

The embedded format seems most suitable when the structured OJT involves learning a task that is performed on or with the assistance of a computer. Many bank tellers acquire the knowledge and skills required to perform various operations directly from their computer screens. The task and the structured OJT are combined in one training medium.

Types of Training

Traditionally, OJT has been perceived as most appropriate for training semiskilled employees to perform technical tasks in production settings (Stokes, 1966). Even today, training a newly hired machine operator through OJT projects a powerful and convincing image to managers. This image is now largely inaccurate. Structured OJT can be used for many other types of training. Most notably, structured OJT can be used successfully for delivering managerial, technical, and awareness training. Table 6.1 defines the three types of training and the associated performance outcomes.

Managerial Training

When structured OJT is used to present managerial training, it gives trainees the ability to plan, direct, or facilitate the efforts of others. These skills enable employees to perform such tasks as resolve conflicts, schedule work activities, facilitate team meetings, and provide feedback. While managerial training does not represent the actual workings of an organization, it is nevertheless important to the organization. Managerial training helps organizations to make the work happen.

The changing nature of jobs means that managerial training is not necessarily restricted to managers and supervisors. It is appropriate for frontline employees as well. Consider that managers and supervisors now receive large amounts of technical training in addition to managerial training. At the same time, frontline hourly employees now receive increasing amounts of managerial training in addition to technical train-

Table 6.1. Types of Training

Training Type	Description	Performance Outcomes
Managerial	Gives the trainee the ability to plan, direct, or facilitate the efforts of others	Verbal or oral skills to ensure that goals are met, projects are completed, and work gets done
Technical	Gives the trainee the ability to manipulate objects, equipment, tools, data, or other resources in some way	Finished products or services, usually tangible in nature
Awareness	Informs the trainee about ideas, processes, or policies presently used in the organization or motivates the trainee to accept planned change in some aspect of the organization	Ability to state ideas in his or her own words or show consistency between words and actions

ing. Indeed, all levels of employees are now likely to receive some type of managerial training.

Here are some titles of structured OJT modules that involve managerial training:

❏ Providing Constructive Feedback
❏ Facilitating Team Meetings
❏ Identifying Customer Requirements
❏ Planning Employee Work Schedules
❏ Conducting a Performance Appraisal.

These titles suggest that managerial training requires that trainees should first understand underlying concepts and principles, often represented as a model or a process, then to apply that information through the use of various communication techniques. Thus, the outcomes of managerial training are often expressed by the oral or written behaviors of trainees.

Technical Training

When structured OJT is used to present technical training, it gives trainees the ability to manipulate objects, equipment, tools, data, or other resources in some way to achieve the training objectives. In general, technical training enables employees to perform a wide variety of tasks ranging from machine operation and document preparation to sales and customer service techniques and safety techniques. Technical training is the most frequent type of training in organizations.

Here are some titles of structured OJT modules that involve technical training:

- Operating the Bolt-Maker Machine
- Inspecting Purchase Order Contracts
- Completing Purchase Order Forms
- Making Contact with Sales Prospects
- Troubleshooting a Financial Audit.

As these titles show, the outcomes that result from technical training are more often than not tangible products or services. To produce these products or services, workers combine psychomotor skills or verbal chains (the linking together of verbal information, such as learning a poem by heart, and so on) with intellectual skills. Many people mistakenly believe that technical training is only about psychomotor skills or verbal chains. In fact, concepts and principles play an important part in technical training. In many cases, concepts and principles are best learned in an off-the-job training program or should be considered prerequisites to the training.

Awareness Training

When structured OJT is used to present awareness training, it can have one or both of two outcomes. The trainee is informed about ideas, processes, or policies that are presently used in the organization, or the employee is motivated to accept some type of planned change in the organization. Because awareness training usually focuses on information rather than on specific job tasks, the outcomes of awareness training are more often cognitive in nature than the outcomes of managerial and technical training. Nevertheless, from the organization's perspective, it is critical for the trainee to have the information.

Here are some titles of structured OJT modules that involve the informational aspect of awareness training:

☐ Knowing Your Health Care Options
☐ Selecting a Profit-Sharing Plan
☐ Understanding Customer Requirements
☐ Understanding the Customer Service Workflow
☐ Knowing Your Role in the Continuous Improvement Process.

Here are some titles of structured OJT modules that involve the motivational aspect of awareness training:

☐ Committing to the New Pull Production System
☐ Working as a Team Member
☐ Using Statistical Process Control (SPC) as a Management Tool
☐ Managing in the New Organization.

At times, managerial training and awareness training may seem indistinguishable. We differentiate them by asking, Does the training content represent information that is directly related to a job expectation? If the answer is yes, the training is likely to be managerial. If the answer is no, the training is likely to be awareness. The importance of this distinction may not be apparent, but type of training does affect the outcomes of training. Managerial training usually requires a trainee to be able to do something as a result of training, while awareness training requires a trainee to know about something at the end of training.

Implications for Structured OJT

The three types of training have important implications for the preparation and delivery of structured OJT modules. We know that a characteristic set of training activities is associated with each type of training. Moreover, these training activities can be organized around a basic instructional pattern, which is often referred to as *whole-part-whole*. Thus, type of training affects the instructional pattern. Table 6.2, adapted from Swanson and Law (1993), shows how the whole-part-whole pattern can be applied to managerial, technical, and awareness training programs.

Table 6.2. Whole-Part-Whole Instructional Pattern

Type of Training	First Whole	Part	Second Whole
Managerial	Purpose Examples Overview of model	Components of model Techniques Decision making	Practice, role play Implications
Technical	Overview of workflow Overview of operation	Start-up procedure Operation procedure Shutdown procedure Inspection procedure	Troubleshooting Practice Integration
Awareness	Problem condition Consequences and opportunities Desired state	Personal actions	Commitment to change

Source: Based on Swanson and Law, 1993.

In practical terms, the whole-part-whole design pattern resembles the dictum: "Tell them what you're going to teach. Teach them. Then tell them what you've taught them." In fact, the whole-part-whole design pattern borrows from at least three different learning perspectives.

The first whole component provides a sense of the big picture or broad context in which the training content is embedded. It also explains the relationship between the broad context and the task or the information to be learned. Hartley and Davies (1976) refer to the techniques used to accomplish the first whole component as *preinstructional strategies*. One of the most well-known of these strategies is the advance organizer introduced by Ausubel (1968). Advance organizers make it possible to learn verbal information through the introduction of related information before the training.

The part component presents the information specific to the learning task. The parts are the details of training, the individual pieces of information that the trainee must master in order to acquire expertise. Learning of the parts can sometimes be facilitated by careful sequencing and by breaking the content down into small logical units. Each unit should be learned individually in order to achieve the entire behavior called for in the training objective. This approach draws on the behavioral learning perspective.

The individual units of training content within the part component can often be sequenced by one of the following principles: simple content to complex content, known content to unknown content, or concrete content to abstract content.

The second whole component connects the individual parts of the training content and shows their relationships. It also promotes insights into the task that is available only as the result of learning the parts. In effect, the second whole gives meaning to the parts through rehearsal or practice. When the trainer requires the trainee to put it all together, he or she asks the trainee to produce behaviors. Producing the behaviors as part of training helps the trainee to learn and retain the information.

The fact that structured OJT relies on experienced employees as trainers gives the whole-part-whole pattern special importance. When experienced employees are left to their own devices, most omit the first whole component. Moreover, when delivering the training, they can omit parts that they mistakenly assume to be obvious or self-evident. Finally, they seldom include the second whole component, since they do not explicitly realize the importance that this information has for others.

As we stated, the whole-part-whole pattern helps to organize training activities for the different types of training. In practice, a single structured OJT lesson can present more than one type of training, which means that some creative programming will be needed. For example, learning why it is important to follow a specific procedure to lock out a piece of equipment is awareness training, but learning the steps of the lockout procedure is technical training. One would seldom train a person on one topic without the other. Logically, learning about safety and learning to do things in a safe way go hand in hand.

Thus, in order for a trainee to have a meaningful learning experience, the training activities that relate to each type of training need to be combined creatively.

Preparation of the Structured OJT Modules

The preparation of a structured OJT module is a matter of combining task information with the appropriate whole-part-whole design pattern into a finished product. Of critical importance is the integration of training content and training events. Depending on the nature of the training content and type of training, this issue can be addressed in either of the two ways described below.

Separate Training Events from Training Content

In some modules, especially modules for technical training, the training events are best separated from the training content. Since technical training usually involves the learning of procedures, decision-making, or troubleshooting information, the training content is often represented in printed form as a job performance guide. As a result, the training events can be presented on a laminated card to be used along with the job performance guide.

In practice, the trainer can decide either to position the card so that it can be referred to throughout the training— for example, by placing it on a clipboard—or to keep the card within reach and use it only as needed. For this reason, we prepare the cards in ways to ensure their flexibility. Sometimes, the card is prepared to fit the shape of a shirt pocket, tool kit, or some other convenient storage location on the trainer or in the job setting.

Embed Training Events in Training Content

In many modules, especially those for managerial and awareness training, it is not appropriate to separate training events from training content. In these modules, the training content is likely to consist of conceptual information as well as of procedures and decision-making or troubleshooting information. When these types of information are combined, we often need to show a close relationship between particular aspects of the training content and the associated training event. As a result, we often need two versions of the structured OJT module: (1) a trainee's version that presents the training content only and (2) a trainer's version that includes both the training content and detailed information based on the five training events used to deliver the content.

As Figure 6.3 shows, embedding the training events in the training content can take the two-column format found in many classroom-based lesson plans. The example is taken from a portion of a structured OJT module on the delegation of work to subordinate employees. The left column presents information for use by the trainer, while the right column presents the training content as seen by the trainee. In this way, the trainer can both present the training content and refer to specific delivery information, such as key words to emphasize in delivery or suggested examples.

To summarize, structured OJT modules serve as the primary reference for trainer and trainee. Thus, judgments about the adequacy of a module should not be based only on its appearance. Expensive binding and color graphics are often unnecessary, and they add to training cost. In fact, training materials that look good all too often end up sitting on a shelf in someone's office and get little actual use. The emphasis needs to be placed not on the form but on the usefulness of training materials.

Conclusion

Structured OJT modules are instructional materials that combine training content with instructions on how to deliver the training. The instructions are based on the five training events. The major components of structured OJT modules are relatively consistent. Structured OJT can be used for three types of training. A whole-part-whole instructional pattern underlies the design of the materials used in all three types of training.

**Figure 6.3.   Example of Training Events
Embedded in the Training Content**

DELEGATING WORK TO SUBORDINATES

1.0. *Prepare the Trainee*

- Review the training objectives with the trainee. Ask the trainee to keep them in mind during the training. Explain that the objectives describe what the trainee should be able to do at the end of the training.

- Emphasize that the task is a major part of the supervisor's job.

- Before going through the list, ask the trainee to come up with at least three ideas of his or her own if a supervisor is unable to delegate effectively.

- Compare the trainee's list and the list presented in the module.

Training Objectives

By the end of this module, you should be able to:

- Describe the process of delegating work to subordinate employees.

- Demonstrate the ability to delegate work to subordinate employees.

Training Rationale

Supervisors must do more than make sure that their employees get their work done. Supervisors must also make sure that employees have the right work to do. Thus, being able effectively to delegate work to others is a critical job requirement of supervisors.

What can happen when supervisors are unable to delegate work to others?

- One or a few people do most of the work, forcing the supervisor to become overly dependent on them and limiting the opportunity to develop other employees.

- Group performance is likely to be hindered if certain employees are absent or doing other tasks.

- Supervisors often feel overwhelmed by the amount of work to be done, especially if only a few employees are doing most of the work.

Prerequisites of the Module

- Review each of the prerequisites.

- Determine whether it is appropriate to continue the training.

You should have done the following before this module:

- Complete the new supervisor orientation program.

- Manage one or more employees for at least one month.

- Have the authority to delegate work to others.

Quality Requirements

- Review the quality require-ments related to the task.

- Emphasize that the company values quality in its products that are sent to customers and quality in the way supervisors interact with subordinates.

Supervisors are expected to keep in mind the following management principles:

- Focus on the performance of employees, not their behavior alone.

- Maintain an employee's self-esteem throughout all interactions.

- Treat each employee fairly.

Training Process

- Make sure that the trainee understands the process.

- Ask whether the trainee has any questions about the information that has been covered so far.

- Clarify any questions before moving on.

The training process is the following:

1. The trainee reviews the module before training begins.

2. The trainer presents the content, allowing the trainee time for practice and to receive feedback.

3. The trainee performs the task at the end of training.

4. The trainer evaluates the trainee's performance.

Getting Ready to Deliver
Structured OJT

WHEN THE TRAINING module has been prepared, the structured OJT is ready to be delivered on demand. The trainer's actions to get ready are part of delivering the structured OJT. This chapter presents the following information:

❑   The training events used for delivering structured OJT
❑   The steps to take when preparing delivery.

Training Events

Chapter Six identified the five training events: prepare the trainee, present the training, require responses, provide feedback, and evaluate performance. This chapter describes them in depth. Training events ensure that the trainer uses the sequence and techniques appropriate to the learning that we want trainees to experience. In other words, training events ensure that trainers use the most effective external activities to bring about the most predictable internal events (Gagne, Briggs, & Wager, 1988).

Today, when companies seek a standard way of delivering OJT, most adopt some variation of the four-step method proposed by Allen during World War I and refined as part of the Training Within Industry (TWI) programs during World War II. The four steps are logical, easy to remember, and effective. Yet, by their very nature, they tend to reinforce the notion that OJT is restricted to the learning of hands-on, technical information. Because the view of expertise in organizations is expanding, we must amend the use of our training events in some essential ways.

Social Learning Theory

At first glance, the five training events may seem to be based more on commonsense logic than on anything else. In fact, they are based on widely accepted principles of social learning theory. Social learning theory assumes that, when individuals are exposed to a model, the stimuli that they receive from the model is coded and retained by them in order to guide the performance of the modeled response (Bandura, 1978). In other words, what trainees remember will become coded instructions to themselves when they attempt later on to reproduce the modeled behavior. The degree of learning is affected by a trainee's attentional, retentional, reproduction, and reinforcement processes.

The paragraphs that follow relate social learning theory to the training events of structured OJT.

Prepare the Trainee. The first event focuses the trainee's attention to the topic at hand, creates an atmosphere conducive to learning, gives meaning to the topic, and establishes standards of performance. Of special importance to structured OJT, this event has been shown to reduce learning anxiety and increase the ability of trainees to learn the training content later on (Gommersall & Meyers, 1966).

Present the Training. The second event serves to guide the attention of trainees toward specific parts of the training content. For these cues to be understood, the trainer needs to make them as visible and as distinct as possible. For this reason, the trainer should separate the content into small components. Trainees can attend more effectively to behaviors that are easily available to them.

Require Responses. The third event calls for trainees to respond in a meaningful way to the model that was presented. Requiring an active response helps trainees to retain content. Rehearsing the modeled behavior enhances retention, because it helps trainees to develop personal codes of the modeled behavior. Also, it helps to expose information that was overlooked during the presentation. In other words, making an active response helps trainees to internalize training content and give it a personal meaning.

Provide Feedback. The fourth event requires the trainer to provide trainees with pertinent information about the accuracy and adequacy of their responses. This information serves to identify the areas in which additional practice and improvement are required. Extensive behavioral research over the past fifty years has formulated some basic principles on the giving of feedback. In general, feedback that is to the point and either immediate or very slightly delayed is preferable in most training situations. Ultimately, a trainee's ability to reproduce the modeled behavior is facilitated by feedback from the trainer.

Evaluate Performance. The fifth training event is a summative judgment of the adequacy of the trainee's performance. The training event gives the trainee a sense of satisfaction by demonstrating that he or she has learned the modeled behavior according to an established standard. This event also ensures that a trainee will consider how the learned behavior transfers to the job. Finally, it ensures that the trainee's performance has undergone a summative judgment by the trainer, which can be documented in the trainee's development plan or personnel record. The quality improvement movement has placed increasing emphasis on the fifth training event.

Training Events and Types of Training

We view the five training events for structured OJT as generic activities. That is, the specific activities to which the events correspond depend on the particular type of training: managerial, technical, or awareness.

Figure 7.1 presents the five training events and the respective actions for each type of training. The training events apply the whole-part-whole instructional pattern described in Chapter Six. In practice, two events present the greatest differences: when the content is presented to the trainee and when the trainee is required to respond. It is not our intent to overcomplicate the seemingly straightforward activity of delivering training content. Rather, our purpose is to show that different types of training require different training designs and that these designs need to be based on the characteristics of the training content. Chapter Eight describes how to use training events to deliver each type of training.

Preparing Delivery

Before structured OJT can be delivered, certain activities have to occur: The training has to be scheduled, training resources have to be secured, and the structured OJT module has to be reviewed. Most of these activities are the responsibility of trainers.

Schedule Training

From the standpoint of supervisors, trainers, and trainees, where and when to conduct the training always seems to pose problems.

Figure 7.1. Training Events and Types of Training

Managerial Training

1. Prepare the trainee

   a. Explain the purpose and rationale of training.
   b. Determine whether the trainee has the prerequisites.
   c. Explain general safety and quality requirements.
   d. Explain how training will be done.
   e. Respond to questions about the training.

2. Present the training

   a. Position the trainee.
   b. Present an overview of the model or process.
   c. Present examples of the model or process in use.
   d. Explain the parts of the model or process.
   e. Demonstrate techniques applying the model or process.
   f. Summarize the entire task.

3. Require a response

   a. Ask the trainee to explain purpose and rationale.
   b. Ask the trainee to describe the model or process.
   c. Ask the trainee for examples of the model or process in use.
   d. Ask the trainee to explain the parts of the model or process.
   e. Ask the trainee to demonstrate techniques.
   f. Ask the trainee to summarize the task.

4. Provide feedback

   a. Inform the trainee about the correctness of responses.
   b. Provide coaching and guidance.
   c. Point out embedded cues in the task setting.

5. Evaluate performance

   a. Evaluate the trainee's self-report.
   b. Evaluate performance test results.
   c. Document the trainee's performance.

(continued)

Figure 7.1. *(continued)*

Technical Training

1. Prepare the trainee

   a. Explain the purpose and rationale of training.
   b. Determine whether the trainee has prerequisites.
   c. Explain general safety and quality requirements.
   d. Explain how training will be done.
   e. Respond to questions about the training.

2. Present the training

   a. Position the trainee.
   b. Present an overview of the operation, equipment, or workflowc. Describe and show each behavior.
   d. Explain specific safety and quality points.
   e. Summarize the entire task.

3. Require a response

   a. Ask the trainee to explain the purpose and rationale.
   b. Ask the trainee to present an overview.
   c. Ask the trainee to explain general safety and quality requirements.
   d. Ask the trainee to describe and show each behavior.
   e. Ask the trainee to explain specific safety and quality points.
   f. Ask the trainee to summarize the entire task.

4. Provide feedback

   a. Inform the trainee about the correctness of responses.
   b. Provide coaching and guidance.
   c. Point out embedded cues in the task setting.

5. Evaluate performance

   a. Evaluate the trainee's self-report.
   b. Evaluate test results.
   c. Document the trainee's performance.

(continued)

Figure 7.1. *(continued)*

Awareness Training

1. Prepare the trainee
   a. Explain the purpose and rationale of training.
   b. Determine whether the trainee has the prerequisites.
   c. Explain general safety and quality requirements.
   d. Explain how training will be done.
   e. Respond to questions about the training.

2. Present the training

   a. Position the trainee.
   b. Present an overview of the topic or issue.
   Inform
   c. Explain the parts of the topic or issue.
   d. Present examples of the topic or issue.
      (Go to 3c)
   Motivate
   e. Describe the present condition and its consequences.
   f. Describe the desired condition and the associated opportunities.
   g. Present examples of the desired condition.
   h. Describe the implications for individuals and the organization.
   i. Discuss commitment behaviors.
      (Go to 3e)

3. Require a response
   a. Ask the trainee to explain the purpose and rationale.
   b. Ask the trainee to present an overview of the topic or issue.
   Inform
   c. Ask the trainee to explain the parts of the topic in his or her own words.
   d. Ask the trainee for examples of the topic.
   Motivate
   e. Ask the trainee to describe the present condition and its consequences
   in his or her own words.
   f. Ask the trainee to describe the desired condition and the associated opportunities.
   g. Ask the trainee for examples of the desired condition.

(continued)

Figure 7.1. *(continued)*

h. Ask the trainee to discuss the implications for self and others.
i. Ask the trainee to describe commitment behaviors.

4. Provide feedback

a. Inform the trainee about the correctness of responses.
b. Provide coaching and guidance.
c. Point out embedded cues.

5. Evaluate performance

a. Evaluate the trainee's self-report.
b. Evaluate the trainee's performance test results.
c. Document the trainee's performance.

Training Location. As we stated in Chapter Three, the nature of the task can dictate where the training is conducted. Structured OJT can sometimes be delivered at the spot where the job is performed, for example, seated before a computer monitor, at the controls of a machine, or at a scheduling board. In other instances, it may not be possible or even necessary to deliver the training where the job is performed.

In the course of identifying the appropriate training location, we have helped some organizations to designate areas within the job setting for the delivery of structured OJT. Much like an instructional carrel, these training stations contain all the equipment, information, and resources that one needs to learn the task in the job setting. These areas are devoted exclusively to structured OJT. They are not for the doing of actual work.

Regardless of where the training occurs, the training location that is selected needs to meet the following criteria:

❑ Provides the same or nearly the same stimuli and context as the spot where the trainee does the job
❑ Does not unduly hinder or inhibit the organization's ongoing production or service delivery activities

❏   Ambient noise, stress, and presence of others who can dis-
    rupt the training are minimal

Any location that meets these criteria can be suitable.
However, we caution against moving too far away from the
spot where the job is done, because that defeats the purpose
of using structured OJT in the first place. As we have emphasized throughout this book, the relevance of training to task
is one of the primary benefits of structured OJT. When structured OJT is delivered away from the actual job setting, the
trainer may have to follow up after training and observe and
coach the trainee on the job.

In many organizations, scheduling involves establishing
the dates of several training sessions. The training schedule
(described in Chapter Six, Figure 6.1) includes the titles of the
training sessions (or phrases defining the job tasks to be
learned), the scheduled training dates, the completion dates,
and the trainer's approval signature. The training schedule
is based on the trainee's development plan.

Training Time. When to deliver the structured OJT is
another important issue. The timing of structured OJT depends on the nature of the task and on constraints during the
workday. Attempting to squeeze both working and training
into the same time period can diminish the effectiveness of
both activities. As a result, some organizations have designated formal time periods for the delivery of structured OJT.
In this way, line managers and supervisors can know who will
be available at certain times of the shift and schedule accordingly. This approach also helps to underline management's
commitment to training as part of the organization's ongoing
business.

In many situations, the most effective training times are
outside normal working hours. At those times, trainers are focused on the training, not on other activities. Also, trainers
sometimes earn extra income by conducting such training.

Finally, trainees may feel less pressure, since they are not disrupting ongoing work. If training is conducted during the workday, we find that shortly after the beginning of the work shift is an effective training time. Trainers and trainees are often at their most alert during this time, and it gives trainees time to practice the knowledge and skills presented in training during the remainder of the shift. It may take only an hour or so for a trainer to present the content, but because some tasks or information require trainees to practice on their own extensively in order to achieve the training objectives, the entire training session may not be completed until the end of the shift.

Training can also be scheduled as part of planned maintenance activities, which may be the only time in which trainees have access to a particular piece of equipment. In this case, scheduling the delivery of structured OJT may have to be coordinated with maintenance or safety departments.

Secure Training Resources

Making certain that all the training resources required are available and making any other arrangements must also precede the delivery of training. Trainers should take the following steps:

❒ Arrange for tools, equipment, documents, forms, or other special resources.
❒ Inform other employees, managers, or supervisors when the training will be conducted.
❒ Eliminate any conflicts over the use of resources required for training.
❒ Schedule a meeting room or work area.

In the broad scheme of organizational priorities, training necessarily ranks lower than work. At the same time, the organization should accommodate requests for training resources. Thus, it is extremely important to make sure that both can go on with a minimal amount of conflict. When resource conflicts do occur, we find more often than not that the root cause is the lack of advance planning on the part of the trainer.

Review the Module

The trainer must also review the training content and the various training events before conducting the training. We advise this for three reasons. First, the module may represent areas of knowledge and skills that the trainer has not used personally for some time. The increased movement toward multi-skilling makes this possibility more likely than the reader may initially expect. Second, the content of the module may have changed in some way of which the trainer is not aware. We are reminded of one instance in which the trainer did not review the module beforehand and was confronted with a significant change in safety procedures of which he had no knowledge. HRD staff had revised the training materials as a result of safety concerns expressed by the safety manager.

Finally, the trainer may require some review on how best to present the information to trainees. For some trainers, review of the module may entail no more than a cursory read-through. For others, review may require a relatively complete rehearsal of the training. The second approach seems important when the task requires the trainee to follow intricate procedures or make complex calculations that may be difficult to replicate each time the training is delivered. Figure 7.2 presents a sample checklist from a structured OJT module. Because the module refers to managerial training, the training can be conducted in a conference room instead of the actual job setting. The module referred to in this checklist utilizes a video program in conjunction with the one-on-one training.

Figure 7.2. Sample Checklist for Getting Ready to Train

Module title: *Delegating Work to Employees*

	Yes	No
Schedule Training		
1. Identify training time with trainee	_____	_____
2. Send Participant's Guide to trainee	_____	_____
3. Schedule conference room	_____	_____
4. Inform trainee's manager of training time	_____	_____
Secure Resources		
5. Gather the following materials:	_____	_____
Notepad and pencils	_____	_____
"Delegating Work Vignettes" videotape	_____	_____
Video playback and monitor	_____	_____
Employee development report form	_____	_____
Review Module		
6. Review contents of module	_____	_____
7. Review training events in module	_____	_____
8. Prepare examples for training	_____	_____
9. Rehearse training delivery	_____	_____

Conclusion

Five training events are used to deliver structured OJT. The exact nature of the events differs for each type of training. The training events increase the chances that trainees will achieve the training objectives. Before delivering structured OJT, a trainer should perform three basic activities in order to get ready.

Delivering Managerial, Technical, and Awareness Training

THE PRIMARY FOCUS in this chapter is how the trainer actually delivers the training. To achieve the intended training objectives, trainers should use the five training events discussed in Chapter Seven to deliver the structured OJT. Instrumental in this chapter is the question:

❐   How is each training event delivered to specific audiences?

Delivering Structured OJT

This chapter focuses on the delivery of structured OJT. We show how to deliver each training event for each type of training. We present this information prescriptively, because our intent is to give the reader a complete understanding of this process. Nevertheless, given the importance of training events, we encourage trainers, after gaining experience, to blend their own individual styles into training delivery. Thus, the reader should not consider our account representative of the one best way of delivering structured OJT.

For example, some experienced trainers have learned to alter the sequence of events or vary the emphasis placed on individual events in order to accommodate the needs of particular trainees. Others have learned how to blend the middle three training events—presentation, response, and feedback—into a seamless, repeating cycle of trainer behavior. Such a blending helps to make the training session like an easygoing but still purposeful social interaction between two individuals, not a stiff formal presentation. We should emphasize that one moves toward such a level of trainer expertise only with a thorough prior understanding of the training events.

Finally, we remind readers that trainers must use effective communication skills. From the beginning of the training session, the trainer should maintain eye contact with the trainee, speak clearly and distinctly, use humor appropriately and only when related to the task, and display positive nonverbal messages. Any trainer should have learned these skills as part of his or her own training and development program.

1. Prepare the Trainee

As Figure 8.1 shows, trainers should perform the same basic five actions for all three types of training. In practice, this training event can occur immediately before the training, a few hours before the training, or even a few days before the training. Sometimes, this training event takes place well before the structured OJT so that the trainee has plenty of time to review the training module. When this training event occurs often depends on the complexity or the difficulty of the task.

In preparing the trainee, the trainer should first explain the purpose and rationale of the training. Often, a rhetorical question helps the trainer to make the point: "Have you ever

Figure 8.1. Prepare the Trainee

Managerial	Technical	Awareness
a. Explain the purpose and rationale of training.		
b. Determine whether the trainee has the prerequisites.		
c. Explain general safety and quality requirements.		
d. Explain how training will be done.		
e. Respond to questions about the training.		

wanted to know what to do when the parts were out of tolerance? Making certain that we send out only good parts is an important part of the operator's job. Our customers depend on the quality of our parts. Well, that's the purpose of this training program. This training program will help you troubleshoot part problems."

Presenting the purpose and rationale in this way, regardless of the type of training involved, helps the trainer to gain the trainee's attention, and it helps the trainee to anticipate what will be presented during the training. It also helps the trainee begin to understand the performance expected as the result of training. The trainer's comments concerning the rationale should link the training with job and organizational outcomes.

Because learning even the simplest task or information requires the trainee to possess some prerequisite knowledge and skills, the next step is for the trainer to verify that the trainee has the necessary prerequisites. The trainer can examine firsthand records of the trainee's past training and work experiences before training begins, or the trainer can now ask the trainee selected questions the answers to which indicate the trainee's existing levels of knowledge and skills. If the trainee does not have all or some of the prerequisites, the trainer can either suspend the training or alter the point at which the training begins in order to accommodate the trainee's entering level of knowledge and skills. Prerequisite knowledge and skills are often more critical for technical and managerial training than they are for awareness training.

Next, the trainer reviews the general safety and quality requirements of the training. In most situations, two levels of safety and quality information can be identified: general safety and quality information related to the task and specific safety and quality information. For example, the trainer should review the basic safety measures associated with working in a certain area—for example, wear goggles or special gloves—or performing an operation—for example, follow the accepted lockout procedure. Quality information can include such things as a review of the company's quality philosophy or customer requirements—for example, "Remember, we don't pass bad parts on to anyone" or "We expect new supervisors to perform all the steps of the performance appraisal process."

The next step in preparing the trainee is to explain how the training will be done. The trainer outlines the steps that will be followed in general terms. The explanation can be as simple as this: "First, I will show you how to do it. Then, I will ask you to repeat the steps back to me. Do you understand?"

Last, answering any questions that the trainee may have can help to increase the effectiveness of training. You may even want to prompt trainees to ask questions about the training. It is common for trainees to display signs of anxiety. They may be fearful of appearing incompetent in front of others, especially if the others have higher status within the organization. The trainer should spend whatever time it takes to put the trainee at ease about the challenges in learning the content. The following suggestions can help the trainer to loosen up the situation:

❐   Make an effort to learn some personal information about the trainee—for example, outside interests, past job experiences, friends in common.
❐   Begin the training session by introducing yourself, asking the trainee to do the same, and following up with some small talk.
❐   Show enthusiasm for the training and the interesting aspects of the task.
❐   Remark that other trainees have felt anxious about training and that they were able to overcome their feelings and learn the task.

2. Present Training

As Figure 8.2 shows, the actions associated with the second training event differ markedly as a result of the type of training being delivered.

Managerial Training. The first step is to position the trainee. The arrangement of trainer and trainee necessarily differs from that in technical training. In managerial training, trainer and trainee usually sit facing each other. The arrangement resembles a conversation much more than it does a demonstration. The trainer may have to indicate explicitly to the trainee where it is best to sit.

Next, the trainer presents an overview of the model or process that defines the task. As stated, managerial training generally requires the trainee first to learn about a model or process, then to learn specific techniques used to apply the model or process. Suppose, for example, that new supervi-

Figure 8.2. Present Training

Managerial	Technical	Awareness
a. Position the trainee.	a. Position the trainee.	a. Position the trainee.
b. Present an overview of the model or process.	b. Present an overview of the operation, equipment, or workflow.	b. Present an overview of the topic or issue.
c. Present examples of the model or process in use.	c. Describe and show each behavior.	*Inform* c. Explain the parts of the topic or issue.
d. Explain parts of the model or process.	d. Explain specific safety and quality points.	d. Present examples of the topic or issue.
e. Demonstrate techniques applying the model or process.	e. Summarize the entire task.	*Motivate* e. Describe the present condition and its consequences.
f. Summarize the entire task.		f. Describe the desired condition and the associated opportunities.
		g. Present examples of the desired condition.
		h. Describe the implications for individuals and organization.
		i. Discuss commitment behaviors.

sors are being trained on the grievance process. The trainer can begin by saying, "Here are the steps of the grievance process that we use here. The process starts at this point, and it ends with a successful resolution at this point. We all work together to make sure that employee issues are addressed fairly."

For a conceptual model, the trainer could say, "This model

shows the relationship between supervisory feedback and employee performance. We believe that appropriate and timely feedback from supervisors can influence how people do their jobs. Have you ever thought that you could influence others in this way?"

At some point, the trainer should present relevant positive and negative examples of the task. This information can be presented before or after the parts of the model or process are presented. A trainer has some discretion in determining the sequence of training actions. In some situations, the trainer might want to begin by asking the trainee to come up with an example: "Tell me about the feedback that you received on your first job? Did you think it was adequate at the time? What was lacking from it?"

Then, the trainer explains the individual parts of the model or process, one by one. Understanding specific parts of the model or process can help the trainee to understand the concepts involved in the task. Those who have written on concept learning, especially Tiemann and Markle (1983), can provide further help in this regard.

Next, the trainer introduces the techniques related to the concepts, often in the form of verbal chains. Knowledge of a process is not very useful if the trainee cannot do something with it. For example, one part of the grievance process that concerns a supervisor is handling conflicts between employees locally before they can become large and expensive issues. Knowledge of the grievance process and of conflict resolution techniques can be considered a single task.

Logically, the trainer's next action is to demonstrate the techniques, using an established set of behaviors. In contrast to technical training, which often requires a trainee to reproduce a behavior exactly as demonstrated, managerial training can accept different behaviors, depending on the individual preferences and experiences of trainers and trainees. But the same criteria should be met no matter what behaviors are used.

Role plays can be extremely effective in demonstrating certain managerial behaviors. In our own work, we have used videotaped scenarios derived from critical incidents (Jacobs, 1986). The trainer should make sure to point out critical aspects shown during the scenarios.

The last step is for the trainer to summarize the training content in its entirety.

Technical Training. Most technical training requires the trainer to demonstrate a set of behavioral actions to the trainee. Thus, the trainer's first action—positioning the trainee to receive the training—is critical. To do so, the trainer may literally have to walk the trainee to the location at which the training will be conducted. Once they have reached the training location, the trainer may have to guide the trainee physically into the most appropriate position. For example, the trainer may have to take hold of the trainee's hands and show the trainee exactly how to hold a tool. The trainer should always make certain that the intent of the action is clear before he or she touches the trainee.

To observe a demonstration, the trainee should be positioned to the side or slightly to the rear of the trainer. In this way, the trainee can view the demonstration from the perspective in which the trainer conducts it. (If the trainee is positioned directly in front of the trainer, he or she has a mirror image, which requires the trainee to interpret the trainer's actions, translate right into left, and so on). Finally, the trainer should avoid placing physical barriers between himself or herself and the trainee. Proper positioning helps to reduce unnecessary hindrances on the trainee's ability to learn. It can be encouraged by phrases such as: "I am going to move you right here so that you can see what I'm doing from a better angle. Don't stand over there, or you won't be able to see everything."

Next, the trainer provides an overview of the operation, piece of equipment, or system workflow in which the task is embedded. The overview specifies where the work comes from, what actions are done at this stage, and who receives the products or services that result from this stage. This information provides a context for the training content that will follow, for example, "As you may know, when the forms get to us, the pricing information for each item has been included on the contract. Our job here is to make sure that all the prices meet our profit requirements. After we're done with the contract, it goes on to sales, which sends it to the customer."

At this point, the trainer can describe and show individual behaviors one by one. During this presentation, the trainee should observe the trainer and, if possible, follow along in the training module. The trainer should always describe the behavior first, often by reading from the training module or having the trainee read what it says. Only then should the trainer demonstrate the behavior. Saying, then doing helps to reinforce the content for the trainee, pace the trainer's disclosure of content, and ensure that key points can be highlighted before the action is taken. The trainer should be prepared to repeat any behavior several times.

As each behavior is presented, the trainer explains any specific quality and safety points associated with it. It is critical for this information to be included in the training module. The trainer should be able to present the behavior and associated quality and safety points as one complete chunk of information.

After presenting all the behaviors, the trainer summarizes the entire task or at least the complete chain of behaviors presented in the demonstration. Most often, this summary is oral. The summary helps the trainee to link the separate behaviors of the task into a meaningful, complete whole. Such linking is especially necessary if the task is complex and if it has to be learned in small bits.

Awareness Training. As in managerial training, the trainer positions the trainee in awareness training as if the two were engaged in conversation. If the awareness training is meant to inform the trainee about information, the trainer should provide an overview of the topic, then cover each of the specific parts of the topic in detail. Here's an example: "This package contains all the information about our profit-sharing plan. There are several details that we will cover today so that you will know how you will be compensated. Let's begin with the first point."

If the awareness training is meant to inform the trainee about an idea, concept, or issue, then the trainer should explain each of its component parts. Relevant examples are often extremely important in awareness training.

When the awareness training is meant to motivate the trainee to form an opinion about something, the trainer approaches the task differently. The trainer begins by describing the present condition in some detail and follows up with examples that help to make the present condition concrete. The trainee may ask the trainee to copy down some of the ideas articulated in the presentation.

Next, the trainer describes the consequences of the present condition, for example, "As you know just by looking around, when we produce a lot of parts at one time, we also make a lot of bad ones. Defects cost the company a lot of money. In the long run, it takes money out of our pockets. Just last month, when we did the large order for Acme Company, we had more than $20,000 in rework costs. Those costs could have been avoided."

Next, the trainer describes the desired condition in some depth and the opportunities that the desired condition can offer. It may be necessary to provide additional examples that help the trainee to understand the desired condition. If the information is new to the organization, the examples may have come from other settings. Then, the trainer discusses the implications for individuals and the organization by moving toward the desired condition. This sequence gives the trainee a basis from which to understand the what, why, and how of the information being presented. Throughout this part of the presentation, the trainer should make sure to present the implications in a fair and objective manner.

Finally, it is important for the trainer to discuss what is required of the trainee in order to make the change occur. This helps to identify the specific behaviors that demonstrate the trainee's commitment to change. Some trainers have used a modified version of Kurt Lewin's force-field analysis technique at this time, as described by Zemke and Kramlinger (1984), to identify the issues that may hinder commitment.

Here is a training sequence that we have used when supervisors were asked to help frontline workers become aware of the organization's change from a push to a pull production system: Supervisors delivered the structured OJT to three or four trainees at a time. Each production approach was introduced, and the consequences of the two approaches were discussed. Soon, in spite of the general conclusion that the pull system would require employees to work harder, employees became comfortable with the change, primarily because they understood what it was and why it was being used.

3. Require Responses

Whenever training is presented, trainees must have opportunities to respond actively. As Figure 8.3 shows, managerial, technical, and awareness types of training require different types of responses.

Managerial Training. In managerial training, when the

Figure 8.3. Require Responses

Managerial	Technical	Awareness
a. Ask the trainee to explain the purpose and rationale.	a. Ask the trainee to explain the purpose and rationale.	a. Ask the trainee to explain the purpose and rationale.
b. Ask the trainee to describe the model or process.	b. Ask the trainee to present an overview.	b. Ask the trainee to present an overview of topic or issue.
c. Ask the trainee for examples of the model or process in use.	c. Ask the trainee to explain general safety and quality requirements.	*Inform* c. Ask the trainee to explain the parts of the topic in his or her own words.
d. Ask the trainee to explain parts of the model or process.	d. Ask the trainee to show and describe each behavior.	d. Ask the trainee for examples of the topic.
e. Ask the trainee to demonstrate techniques.	e. Ask the trainee to explain specific safety and quality requirements.	*Motivate* e. Ask the trainee to describe the present condition and its consequences in his or her own words.
f. Ask the trainee to summarize the learning task.	f. Ask the trainee to summarize the entire task.	f. Ask the trainee to describe the desired condition and the associated opportunities.
		g. Ask the trainee for examples of the desired condition.
		h. Ask the trainee to discuss the implications for him- or herself and others.
		i. Ask the trainee to describe commitment behaviors.

trainer prompts the trainee to respond, he or she asks the trainee to repeat the purpose and rationale of the training. Then, the trainer asks the trainee to explain the model or process. Next, the trainer asks the trainee either to give some examples of how the model or process is used or to respond to examples that were not presented in the training.

The trainer expects the trainee to state why specific examples do or do not suit the concept defined during training. For example, the trainer can introduce a subordinate feedback model that lacks at least one critical attribute. The trainee should be able to identify the missing attribute and state the consequences that its absence can have on a subordinate's performance. Then, the trainee should explain the parts of the model or process in a meaningful way.

Possibly the most important aspect of the trainee's responses is his or her ability to demonstrate that he or she can use the related techniques appropriately. To this end, the trainer can suggest that they engage in a role play in which the trainee demonstrates the technique. No matter how the techniques are demonstrated, the trainer must be certain to elicit all possible variations of the desired responses from the trainee.

Finally, the trainer asks the trainee to summarize the entire task.

Technical Training. Presumably, the opportunity to observe the trainer explain and demonstrate the task prepares the trainee to explain and demonstrate the same task. The trainer usually begins by prompting the trainee, for example, "Okay, now it's your turn to show me. I want you to tell me the purpose of the task and why it is important. Then, I want you to tell and show me how to do each step, including all the quality and safety points along the way."

The trainer should also tell the trainee to what extent he or she can use the training module during the response. In most instances, the trainee should be able to use the module whenever required, since it was not intended for the trainee to memorize its content. Throughout the trainee's response, the trainer prompts the trainee to respond in specific ways determined by the training objective. It may be necessary to have the trainee restate the general safety and quality requirements of the task at this time.

For several reasons, it is important to have the trainee first describe, then perform the response. First, such a sequence allows the trainer to step in if the trainee proposes to perform an action that is unsafe or that would have harmful consequences. Also, such a sequence may further reinforce the content, since it calls on two independent response modes. Finally, because some responses may have to be simulated—for example, removal of a part that cannot actually be touched—trainers always have at least one way of determining whether the trainee has learned the content.

Depending on the size of the task, the trainer may not wait until all the training content has been presented. Instead, the trainer may decide to separate the content into logical chunks and require the trainee to respond at the end of each chunk. Within the context of the response, the trainee includes the safety and quality information related to the particular chunk. Finally, the trainer may want to have the trainee link the various parts of the content together into one continuous response set. Often, this linking can be done verbally.

Awareness Training. For both forms of awareness training, the trainee's response requirements are relatively straightforward. The trainee should provide a brief overview of the topic and then describe each part of the topic. It may be necessary to have the trainee conclude by summarizing the content of the training. The trainer should encourage the trainee to use the words that are most meaningful to him or her.

When awareness training is used to inform, the trainee should be required first to explain the topic or issue in his or her own words, then to give original examples of the topic of training. When awareness training is used to motivate trainees to form an opinion, the response requirements are necessarily more involved. In the appropriate wording, the trainee should be asked first to describe the present condition, then to discuss some consequences of the present condition in depth. Next, the trainee should be asked to produce some examples of the desired condition. Finally, the trainer should ask the trainee to discuss the implications of the desired condition for the trainee, for other employees in the trainee's work area, and perhaps also for the organization as a whole. In this way, trainer and trainee can begin to discuss the actions that the trainee should take to achieve the desired condition. After the trainee has stated the value of the desired condition and reconciled the implications, the trainer should attempt to obtain statements that the trainee is committed to achieving the desired situation.

The trainer should not try to coerce the trainee into making statements that are harmful or counter to the trainee's actual beliefs. Rather, the statement of commitment helps to bind the trainee to the new ideas, and it suggests behaviors that the trainee can take in accordance with the commitment.

4. Provide Feedback

As Figure 8.4 shows, all three types of training require the same basic actions from the trainer. The trainer should give feedback based on an objective assessment of the adequacy of the trainee's response. The behavioral sciences literature has well documented the potency of feedback on learning. Feedback has been shown to have even greater impact when the persons involved have differing levels of status. The relationship between trainer and trainee often involves such a

Figure 8.4. Provide Feedback

Managerial	Technical	Awareness
	a. Inform about the correctness of responses. b. Provide coaching and guidance as required. c. Point out embedded cues in the task setting.	

status differential, which can be based on differences in formal job roles or simply on the respect that people tend to give to those who have demonstrated their expertise in a particular topic.

The first step of this training event is to inform the trainee about the correctness of his or her response. The feedback should be given immediately or very soon after the response. Unless the trainee's response involves harmful consequences, the trainer should refrain from giving feedback while the trainee responds. Interrupting a response can deform it and diminish the trainee's sense of achievement. There is no standard way of phrasing or delivering feedback, but the trainer should strive to be specific about the elements of the response that were correct and the elements that were not correct. Feedback should be both positive and negative.

The next step of this training event is to provide coaching and learning guidance when appropriate. If a large number of the trainee's responses are incorrect and it is obvious that the trainee cannot possibly make correct responses on his or her own, then the trainer may have to repeat the training, this time reducing the size of individual chunks of the training content. The trainee can be asked to respond at the conclusion of each chunk. However, if the trainee makes few incorrect responses or if the errors are concentrated in a few areas, the trainer can elect to coach the trainee in order to achieve the correct responses (Fournies, 1978). That is, the trainer provides a continuous set of behavioral prompts focused on relatively small parts of the training content, and the trainee responds immediately.

While it is important for the trainer to provide the trainee with feedback and coaching, not all the feedback should come from the trainer. The trainer should help trainees to identify independent sources of feedback embedded in the task itself. For some tasks, such as making an adjustment to the height of a press ram or using a sales technique on a prospective buyer, the feedback is automatic. In both of the cases just cited, the trainee can observe the immediate effects of these actions, which in effect are independent sources of feedback. For that reason, the trainer should include in his or her feedback information about where the trainer can look for feedback on his or her own. Feedback is often more effective when it comes from sources that tell the trainee directly whether his or her response is correct without necessarily involving others.

5. Evaluate Performance

As Figure 8.5 shows, the fifth training event requires the trainer to use trainee self-reports and objective performance tests to determine whether the trainee has in fact achieved the intended training objective. The trainer considers the information available, then documents the decision in the trainee's development plan or similar personnel record.

The term *trainee self-report* refers to the trainee's own evaluation of his or her learning progress. To gather such information, the trainer should ask the trainee to reflect critically on what he or she has accomplished and on the areas in which he or she may require additional practice. A trainer

Figure 8.5. Evaluate Performance

Managerial	Technical	Awareness
	a. Evaluate the trainee's self-report. b. Evaluate performance test results. c. Document the trainee's performance.	

should not be coy. For example, you can ask directly, "Do you feel that you have achieved the objective? Do you think you can now perform the task on your own? What areas of the task are still unclear to you?"

In interpreting a trainee's self-evaluation, the trainer may wonder whether the trainee is giving an honest opinion or merely a response that he or she believes to be socially acceptable. After all, the trainee may not want to disappoint the trainer, regardless of the truth of the matter. Nevertheless, research tends to support the notion that adults can and will assess their own learning progress accurately, even if the assessment is to their disadvantage. Recent studies on self-directed learning have shown that adults are capable of wisely selecting learning activities to address their internal and external development needs. Moreover, studies on learner-controlled instruction conducted during the 1960s and 1970s found no significant differences in achievement between trainees who were permitted to skip over content that self-assessment indicated they had already learned and trainees who were required to complete all the content.

The term *performance test* refers to the trainer's judgment of the adequacy of the trainee's responses. The trainer bases the judgment on standards that refer to the training objective. To gather this information, the trainer uses performance-rating scales or cognitive tests. Performance-rating scales require a trainer to observe the trainee's actions or the result of the trainee's actions and then give a partial and an overall rating.

Cognitive tests, such as multiple-choice tests and completion tests, can also help the trainer to evaluate the trainee's performance. In practice, cognitive tests are limited in their ability to measure job performance, and thus they are less useful than performance-rating scales for most structured OJT situations. Cognitive tests can be useful in testing the attainment of concepts and principles associated with awareness training.

The issues of reliability and validity invariably arise whenever a trainer evaluates a trainee. In relative terms, validity is of less concern than reliability, since the high relevance of structured OJT ensures that training objectives match job expectations. However, reliability raises two basic questions. First, would two or more trainers evaluate the same behavior in the same way? Second, would the same trainer evaluate similar behaviors in different trainees in the same way? These two questions can be addressed through a thorough training and development program for trainers and through ongoing monitoring of the trainers.

Finally, the trainer completes the training by reaching a summative judgment about the trainee's performance. This judgment is based on self-reports and performance tests. As we have stated, this information documents that the trainee has completed the training. In an increasing number of organizations, the trainer's evaluation leads to formal certification in performance of the task for the trainee.

Conclusion

This chapter has shown how to deliver structured OJT for the three types of training. The five training events provide a time-tested method for ensuring effective training. In practice, structured OJT seldom occurs in the same way for every trainee. Some trainees require relatively small chunks of content before responding, while others can handle large chunks. The trainer makes the judgment while delivering the training. Training seldom occurs in a straight, linear path. Usually, some steps need to be repeated.

CHAPTER 9

Evaluating and Troubleshooting Structured OJT

THE LAST STEP of the structured OJT process is to evaluate and troubleshoot the training. Of course, in a practical sense, evaluating and troubleshooting are continuous, ongoing activities in any system. This chapter presents:

❐ Questions that should be asked to evaluate structured OJT
❐ How to troubleshoot training system components and issues arising from the organizational context.

Evaluation Questions

Many authors (for example, Brinkerhoff, 1987; Robinson & Robinson, 1989; Dixon, 1990) have addressed the evaluation of human resource development activities. In this chapter, we focus on the questions used to evaluate structured OJT. The model that we introduced in Chapter Two provides a framework specific for organizing the question. That is, the questions that should be asked are based on the system components of outcomes, processes, and inputs. We also need to ask

139

questions about the environment—in this case, the organization—in which the system resides.

Figure 9.1 presents a list of questions related to system components and organizational context. It is common in evaluation to establish desired performance standards for each question and then to compare actual performance with standards. In that way, we can determine the value and worth of each component of the system and of the entire system as a whole. We assume that an evaluation that asks these questions will be conducted by a team of employees who are knowledgeable in the use of evaluation methods, perhaps with assistance from outside consultants.

The remainder of this section discusses the evaluation questions outlined in Figure 9.1. Where appropriate, we provide additional information based on our experience. The reader should note that we begin our discussion with training outputs, since these are critical when we evaluate systems. It makes no sense to ask, say, whether the training was conducted properly if the training objectives have not been met. In a truly effective system, both questions should be answered affirmatively.

Training Output Questions

Training output questions focus on the various effects of having used structured OJT. These questions look at what is left after the training has been completed. Following are some possible areas of focus of output questions:

❑ Training objectives
❑ Trainee's development goals
❑ Organizational goals
❑ Unanticipated effects of training.

Training output questions usually raise the most interest

Figure 9.1. Structured OJT Evaluation Questions

Training Outputs

1. Were the training objectives achieved?
2. What were the effects on job performance? on organizational performance?
3. Were the training outcomes consistent with the trainee's development needs?
4. Were there unanticipated effects?

Training Process

1. How much time did it take to conduct the training?
2. Was the training location adequate? Were the needed resources available?
3. Did the trainer get ready to train?
4. Did the trainer use the module as intended?
5. Did the trainer use the training events as intended?
6. Did the trainer document the training as expected?
7. Did the trainer use effective communication skills?
8. Did the trainee use the module as instructed?
9. Did the trainee attend to the trainer?
10. Did the trainee ask questions?
11. Did the trainee like the content/training approach?

Training Inputs

1. Was the learning task appropriate?
2. Was the learning task analyzed adequately?
3. Was the module accurate and complete and appropriately formatted?
4. Was the training design appropriate?
5. Were training resources available in the training location?
6. Was the training location suitable for the delivery of training?
7. Did the trainee have the prerequisites needed for training?
8. Did the trainee have the personality or learning style suitable for structured OJT?
9. Was the most appropriate experienced employee selected as trainer?

(continued)

Figure 9.1. *(continued)*

10. Did the experienced employee receive adequate training and development experiences?

Organizational Context

1. Did management provide sufficient resources to support the structured OJT?
2. Can the structured OJT occur within the constraints of the production or service delivery schedule?
3. Do labor-management contractual agreements allow employees to participate as trainers?
4. Are staffing levels sufficient to allow experienced employees to take time to train others?

---

among system stakeholders. Simply put, if a senior manager wants proof that structured OJT works, the output questions provide the basis for a response.

The training output question that is usually asked first is whether training objectives have been met. As we stated in Chapter Eight, the trainer's use of performance-rating scales and cognitive tests does much to address this evaluation question in the short term. In the long term, this question can be addressed by interviewing trainees at specified intervals after training, by interviewing supervisors, or by reviewing performance records. Given the planned nature of structured OJT, it is highly likely that the intended objectives of training will be achieved.

It may also be important to determine whether training objectives were consistent with the trainees' development goals. While it is important to show that structured OJT achieves the training objectives, it may be equally important to determine whether training met the needs of trainees. For a training program to be truly effective, it should be viewed as a means to achieve organizational and individual goals.

However, the individual goals have to be expressed beforehand, and they have to be articulated with the needs of the organization.

For most managers, the bottom line in structured OJT is its effect on the effort to achieve business goals. Training objectives should be linked with measures of job or group performance during the analysis that precedes the design of structured OJT. The business goals are the reason for conducting the training in the first place. Unfortunately, while this bottom-line aspect of training evaluation has generated much interest and attracted much attention, for a variety of reasons it is seldom addressed in organizations. A few notable exceptions exist, including a study of OJT and work performance measures by Kainen, Begley, and Maggard (1983). Our own work has sought to address the management impact question by examining the effects of structured OJT and unstructured OJT. The financial forecasting models and related tools that allow bottom-line evaluations to be achieved with a high degree of confidence can now be found in the literature (Swanson & Gradous, 1988).

Our research has focused on two basic questions. First, we have sought to determine whether the outcomes of structured OJT and of unstructured OJT differ in quality.

Do employees who receive structured OJT perform a task better than employees who receive another kind of training?

Second, we have sought to determine whether one kind of training is more efficient than the other.

Does structured OJT achieve the objectives faster than other training approaches and, if it does, what are the financial implications?

The performance time graph shown in Figure 9.2 has guided much of our thinking on the evaluation of job and organizational outcomes. The key question is this: Does it make good economic sense to invest in structured OJT as opposed to other forms of training, such as unstructured OJT, even though its costs are higher?

Our research has consistently shown that structured OJT is superior to unstructured OJT in training situations in which a performance need has been demonstrated. Employees who learn tasks through structured OJT make fewer quality errors than employees who learn through unstructured OJT. The reduction in errors had been shown to have a substantial financial impact on organizations. For example, the financial benefits of reducing the quality errors for a single assembly task over one year have been calculated at $24,000 (Jacobs, 1994). In addition, employees achieve training objectives faster and more completely through structured OJT than through unstructured OJT. The increased efficiency and thor-

Figure 9.2. Learning Times for Unstructured and Structured OJT

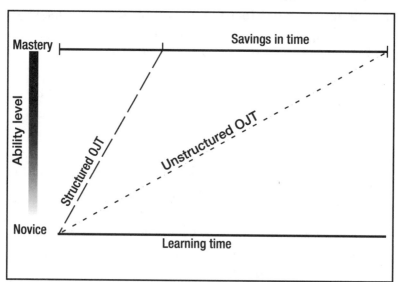

oughness have been shown to have financial benefits. For example, an organization that increased training efficiency by a factor of five times through the use of structured OJT received twice the financial benefits in terms of employee productivity (Jacobs, Jones, & Neil, 1992).

We urge the reader to try to address similar questions whenever possible in your own organization. The techniques may at first seem complicated, or the data required to conduct the analyses may be difficult to obtain. Despite the difficulties involved, however, the results can have important payoffs. Few evaluation questions have the same degree of relevance and meaning for an organization's leaders and managers when you have to justify the use of structured OJT.

Finally, structured OJT can have unanticipated positive effects. For example, the following outcomes have been observed regarding structured OJT:

☐ Empower employees to become part of the ongoing activities of their work areas. Employees come to have a greater stake in the outcomes that are produced by all.

☐ Increase the perception among employees that the organization cares about their progress and that it is willing to commit scarce resources to this end.

☐ Remove some of the fears and anxieties that employees have about learning a new task. Learning should not be a test. Rather, learning should be made as easy as possible.

☐ Provide managers a means of observing promising frontline employees and assessing their potential promotion. It requires employees to accept responsibility and authority, and it fosters self-direction and confidence. How individual employees respond to these challenges are important to management.

☐ Distribute responsibility for the development of expertise throughout the organization while maintaining that the ultimate accountability lies with management and the individual employee.

☐ Become part of the organization's ongoing continuous improvement efforts, since jobs and tasks are being scrutinized by those who actually do the work.

☐ Increase discussion among employees about the one best way of doing something and diminish the variations in individual practice. It requires employees to begin to reflect on how they do their work.

☐ Provide the HRD staff a distinct role. Before structured OJT is introduced, it seems likely that their influence on how OJT was conducted within their organization was limited. HRD staff should help to design and manage structured OJT.

☐ Increase the transfer of specific job information between departments, such as between engineering and production, and between locations at which similar work is being done.

☐ Ensure that everyone is being trained to do a job or task in the same way. Standardization of work practices becomes a basis for certifying employees to perform jobs in compliance with ISO 9000 requirements.

☐ Provide a basis for high work standards in work areas. The same criteria can be applied to all employees.

Training Process Questions

Training process questions focus on the behaviors of trainer and trainee during training. They ask how the structured OJT was carried out and how the content was learned. While process questions may have less interest for managers than output questions, they provide valuable insights into the workings of training. Answering process questions usually requires observation during training and interviews after training. To ensure that the observational data that are gathered are consistent, standardized forms that measure the frequency of the trainer's and the trainee's behaviors need to be developed.

The general questions about the training process address such issues as the amount of time required to complete training. It is also important to know whether the resources needed for training were in fact available during training. Finally, questions can be asked about the suitability of the job setting to the delivery of training.

Evaluation questions about the trainer's behavior ask whether the trainer did all that was necessary to get ready for the training, how the trainer used the training module and the training events, and whether the trainer followed by completing all ratings and personnel forms as expected. We also ask whether the trainer used effective communication skills.

While learning occurs within individuals, we can make inferences about learning progress by observing outward behaviors. The process questions about the trainee's behavior ask whether the trainee used the module as instructed by the trainer. We are interested in the attending behavior of the trainee, that is, how the trainee responded to the trainer during the training. We want to know what kind of questions the trainee asked during the training. And finally we want to know how the trainees felt about the content and process of the structured OJT. Some people downplay the role of attitudes and feelings, but at the very least, knowing how a trainee feels about his or her training process can help an organization chart that trainee's later course of action.

Training Input Questions

Training input questions focus on the system components present at the time of the training: learning task, training module and training design, training location, trainee, and trainer. As we explain in the next section of this chapter, many, if not all, of the problems associated with the use of structured OJT can be traced back to the absence of some input component. Answering evaluation questions about training input usually requires us to conduct interviews.

Questions about the learning task ask whether it was appropriate for structured OJT and whether it was analyzed adequately. While the training module and the training design that it reflects are clearly system inputs, it may be possible to gather information about them by asking questions about the process. For example, determining whether the module format was appropriate or the training sequence was logical may depend on obtaining information from the trainee and trainer during training.

Questions about the job setting focus on the availability of training resources and on the overall suitability of the job setting as a training location. Many issues about the use of the job setting for training should have been resolved when the training location was selected. However, it is reasonable to assume that all issues cannot be anticipated and that it is therefore appropriate to ask such questions after training as well.

The amount of time invested in evaluation questions about trainee and trainer can depend on the effectiveness of prior planning activities. Clearly, it is not appropriate to allow a trainee who lacks the prerequisites or the personality required for training to attend training. Clearly, it is not appropriate to allow an inexperienced employee or an employee who has not received adequate training and development to conduct training. But insights such as these about specific situations may not emerge until after the fact.

Organizational Context Questions

In Chapter Two, we stated that structured OJT always exists

in an organizational context. No evaluation of structured OJT can be considered complete until we determine how the context affected the training. Possibly the most critical issue is the extent of management commitment to the use of structured OJT. Structured OJT requires at least as much commitment as off-the-job training approaches, if not more. Commitment means that individuals behave in ways that are consistent with their stated beliefs (Dowling, 1992).

We have seen senior managers insist that they are committed to the use of structured OJT and then waver when confronted with the realities of such a commitment. For example, it is often necessary to provide replacements for experienced employees who take time off the job to prepare and conduct training. And tools and equipment may have to be purchased for training. Managers should show their commitment by being willing to examine the organization's culture and structure and by determining the changes that have to be made in order to accommodate structured OJT. Structured OJT cannot be expected to stand alone. Management commitment is critical to change. Managers must be encouraged to walk their talk on this issue if structured OJT is to be effective.

Another key issue is the way in which structured OJT interacts with other systems in the organization, both positively and negatively. Structured OJT interacts with such other organizational systems as:

❏ Production or service delivery
❏ Employee development
❏ Labor-management relations
❏ Employee recruitment and selection.

For structured OJT to be effective, it must harmonize with the other systems around it. That is, the goals of one system must be consistent with the goals of the other system. When supervisors complain that structured OJT is interfering with their ability to get work done, they mean that the goals of the two systems—structured OJT and production—are in conflict.

To summarize, the evaluation questions listed in Figure 9.1 are meant to frame the evaluation of structured OJT. Once the evaluation information has been gathered and conclusions about the results have been drawn, the task at hand is to troubleshoot the system.

Troubleshooting Structured OJT

In general, when systems do not achieve their intended goals, we determine why by examining the system components. Examining the information available and deducing the most likely causes enables us to select solutions that will be effective in correcting the problem. The same approach can be used in troubleshooting structured OJT. That is, when a structured OJT program does not achieve the intended training outputs, we determine why by examining its system components. We can troubleshoot structured OJT at two levels of analysis: the training system level and the organizational level.

Training System Level

The training system level of analysis focuses on the components of the training system. To determine why one or more of the training outputs was not achieved as expected, we examine each of the training system components. In order for structured OJT to achieve the desired outputs, the components must be both adequate and complete.

Training Inputs. In many instances, structured OJT fails to achieve the intended outputs because one of the training inputs is faulty. For example, we may have the right trainee and the right trainer, but the location selected for the training was not appropriate. Asking the questions that follow will help to determine whether the cause of the problem exists in the training inputs.

Is the cause related to the trainee?
1. Did the trainee have the prerequisites?
2. Did the trainee have the personality suited for this training approach?

Is the cause related to the trainer?
1. Did the trainer have sufficient knowledge and skills in the learning task?
2. Did the trainer have the knowledge, skills, and attitude needed to be a trainer?

Is the cause related to the training location?
1. Were the necessary training resources available?
2. Were there scheduling conflicts with ongoing production or service delivery?
3. Was the atmosphere conducive to training and learning?

Is the cause related to the learning task?
1. Was the task suitable for structured OJT?
2. Was the task analyzed adequately?
3. Was the module prepared adequately?

Training Process. The training process describes the way in which the structured OJT was carried out. Trainers, often with the best of intentions, sometimes alter the training content or the training delivery in some way, or they deliver the training in different ways to individual trainees. These changes can affect training outputs in unpredictable ways. Asking the following questions will help to determine whether the cause of the problem exists in the training process:

1. Was the trainer ill-prepared for his or her presentation(s) of training material?

2. Was the training content incomplete?
3. Was the delivery of training ineffective or lacking in focus?
4. Was the trainee's performance inadequately tested at the end of training?

Training Outputs. Looking for the cause of problems in training outputs is to question the validity of training goals. This is not as implausible as it may sound. Structured OJT closely links training objectives and job expectations. If job expectations change during the design process, training objectives also have to change. If they do not, training is likely to fail. Asking the following questions will help to determine whether the cause of the problem exists in the training outputs:

1. Did job expectations change?
2. Did the trainee's development and goals change?
3. Did the requirements of other organizational systems change?

To summarize, problems can be caused by missing or inadequate training system components. The solution depends on the cause of the problem. For example, if the cause is determined to be inconsistency in the delivery of training, one solution is to give trainers a mnemonic device, such as a sticker, that reminds them to use the training events in the order prescribed in the training module. Effective solutions that are simple and low in cost are always preferable. Yet we also need to state that, if the structured OJT process is followed, very few remedial solutions should be required.

Organizational Level
Unfortunately, the causes of problems associated with structured OJT are not all located at the training system level. We say *unfortunately,* because causes at the training system level are relatively easy to fix. The causes can also lie at the orga-

nizational level. Issues that affect structured OJT from the organizational context are far more difficult to fix. Asking the following questions will help to determine whether the cause of the problem exists in the organizational context:

1. Does the structured OJT conflict with business issues or priorities that face the organization faces as a whole?
2. Does the structured OJT conflict with ongoing change efforts within the organization?
3. Do management, supervisors, or frontline employees place relatively low value on training?
4. Do present agreements between management and unions inhibit structured OJT?
5. Are the goals of training aligned with the goals of related organizational systems?
6. Are the job expectations of experienced employees aligned with the role of being a structured OJT trainer?
7. Are line or staff functions within the organization unwilling to provide the support necessary to manage the structured OJT after it has been implemented?

Clearly, the nature of the issues just reviewed makes it unrealistic that managers or HRD professionals acting alone can resolve them in substantive ways. Nevertheless, it can be important to determine which issues are affecting structured OJT, since the resulting information can spur creativity to get around the roadblocks stemming from the organization. For example, we have helped managers and union officials to find a compromise that allows experienced employees to act as trainers and that maintains the spirit of the original contractual agreement.

Indeed, the troubleshooting of problems whose causes lie in the organizational context usually requires more time and political savvy than the troubleshooting of problems created by training system components. Nevertheless, when the individuals involved understand and value the contributions that structured OJT can make, it is likely that meaningful actions can be taken, even if issues cannot be addressed directly. In many instances, identifying the issues at least gives the parties involved a concrete focus for creative troubleshooting.

Conclusion

The last step of the structured OJT design process is to evaluate and troubleshoot the actual training. Evaluation is framed by questions focused on system outputs, processes, and inputs. Evaluation also needs to address the organizational context in which structured OJT occurs. For this reason, we troubleshoot structured OJT both at the training system level and at the organizational level.

PART THREE

Using Structured OJT

The chapters in Part Two described the steps of the structured OJT process. However, one does not arrive at a successful product simply by performing these steps. The chapters in Part Three examine the context in which structured OJT takes place. The use of structured OJT usually involves change, and we can improve the chances of success by thinking of structured OJT as a change process that can be managed. Managing the change process helps to ensure that structured OJT will be successful. Chapter Ten examines the change process and addresses issues often raised when the use of structured OJT is first proposed. In Chapter Eleven, we appeal for the development of a culture of expertise within organizations. Structured OJT is likely to play a major role in the development both of the culture and of the expertise.

CHAPTER 10

Managing the Change Process and Issues in the Use of Structured OJT

THE INDIVIDUAL STEPS of the structured OJT process are only part of the success of structured OJT. Managing the change process is equally important. The topics addressed in this chapter are:

❒ Defining the change management process for structured OJT
❒ Issues of concern in the use of structured OJT.

Change Management Process

We would be remiss if, on the basis of the preceding chapters, the reader believed that using the structured OJT process was all that it took to produce a successful training program. While the process shows how to design, deliver, and evaluate structured OJT, it does not guarantee that the organization will accept this training approach. Our view is that we need to view the use of structured OJT from a change management perspective. This perspective states that both the organization and structured OJT are systems and that the two systems have to be reconciled if they are to achieve mutually dependent goals. Without this perspective, structured OJT is likely to be short-lived.

Figure 10.1, based on a model of organization development by Cummings and Worley (1993), shows the change management process for structured OJT. The process essentially treats the structured OJT as a pilot project having a starting point and ending point and a goal of institutionalizing the use of structured OJT in the long term. The change management process seems appropriate for use regardless of whether the structured OJT is introduced by an internal employee, most likely the HRD manager, or an external consultant. Either party can be considered part of the team, responsible for facilitating the improvement process in the organization. The change management process has four steps: entering and contracting, diagnosing the pilot area, implementing the pilot study, and evaluating and revising. The remainder of this section examines these four steps.

Entering and Contracting

The first step of the change has two stages: entering into negotiation and developing the contract with the client.

Entering. The entering stage is intended to determine the fit between structured OJT and the organization and whether the organization is prepared to commit the necessary re-

Figure 10.1. Change Management Process

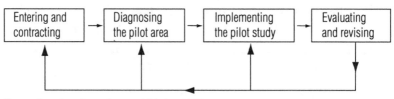

Source: Based on Cummings and Worley, 1993.

sources to ensure success. In Chapters Two and Nine, we suggested that structured OJT systems are affected by issues arising in the organizational context. The entering stage helps to identify the issues that have the most importance and to predict their likely effects on a structured OJT program. Management can then decide whether or not to proceed.

The entering stage usually involves meeting with senior managers from a number of different areas, including production, human resources, safety, and engineering, to discuss the problems and opportunities that confront the organization. These meetings are critical, since they provide a sense of the organization's readiness for change. Some have referred to these activities as courtship, since each party is looking at the other as a potential partner, and no commitment is made until both parties have gathered adequate information.

The following questions summarize key indicators that can determine whether structured OJT fits the organization:

- ❏ Is senior management willing to commit resources to support structured OJT?
- ❏ Are managers and supervisors willing to host a structured OJT pilot project in their work area?
- ❏ Are off-site training programs already present in the organization? Are they valued?
- ❏ In what ways could structured OJT address the organization's most pressing needs?
- ❏ What priorities do senior executives express for human resources?
- ❏ Have contractual agreements between union and management been altered to reflect a desire to use structured OJT?
- ❏ Have internal planning committees been established to review the feasibility of using structured OJT and address any issues that may inhibit its use?

❑   Have line and staff managers called in internal memos for changes in training policies?

❑   What kind of ongoing change efforts, such as safety awareness or continuous quality improvement programs, are already in place? Can structured OJT play a role in the existing programs?

❑   Is the human resource development department or are other logical functional areas willing to manage the structured OJT program?

The feasibility of proceeding with the project can be determined from the answers to these questions.

It is reasonable to expect that structured OJT will not be appropriate in some organizations. In fact, information that emerged during the entering stage has led us to walk away from more than one organization that was interested in using structured OJT but which was deficient in some aspect that would have made the success of a structured OJT project unlikely. The specific issues that can hinder the project should be clearly identified for the client.

Contracting. If structured OJT does seem feasible for the organization, the second stage is to develop a contract specifying the particulars of the project. Developing a contract is often an iterative process whereby the contract is revised repeatedly to ensure that the language suits all parties. Even if the specific location has not been selected for the pilot study, it is often possible for the contract to specify the broad functional area, such as customer service, retail sales, or maintenance, that will host the structured OJT project.

The contract should spell out the following items of the project:

❑   Goals
❑   Deliverables
❑   Probable pilot study areas

❐ Roles of individuals inside and outside the organization
❐ Financial, physical, and human resources that the organization will provide in support
❐ Evaluation criteria
❐ Consultant costs
❐ Timeline
❐ Renegotiation statement.

Diagnosing the Pilot Area

The next step of the change management process is to conduct a detailed study of the problems or issues that affect specific functional areas within the organization and to select a specific location for the pilot study.

In general, an in-depth analysis of the organization requires problems within functional areas to be documented in terms of the present levels of performance and the desired levels of performance. Unfortunately, managers are often not able to provide group or individual performance information in this way. As we have stated, structured OJT should be used only when a documented performance problem caused by lack of knowledge, skills, or attitudes has been determined to be the cause of the problem. For this reason, the diagnosis stage may have to include a performance analysis. If it does, the contract agreement may have to be renegotiated. Having performance information framed in terms of present level and desired level is especially critical for the success of a project.

Documenting the performance problems is likely to reveal one or more potential locations for the pilot study. A pilot study resembles full-scale implementation, but it is limited to specific areas. We use the following criteria to select the locations for structured OJT pilot studies:

❐ The interest of area managers and supervisors in hosting a pilot study and their readiness to do so

❏   The interest of frontline employees in those areas in partici-
     pating in the pilot project
❏   The representativeness of the work being done in those
     areas
❏   The consequences of the problems and documented by per-
     formance analysis for those areas
❏   The overall chance of success in implementing structured
     OJT in those areas.

As part of the diagnosis step, key individuals may be
asked to provide an overview of structured OJT to managers,
supervisors, union leaders, and other key stakeholders within
the potential pilot study locations. The overviews of structured OJT that we prepare for management usually follow this
order:

1.   Define *structured OJT* and *unstructured OJT.*
2.   Provide examples of structured and unstructured OJT.
3.   Describe the benefits of structured OJT.
4.   Describe the general steps of an action plan.
5.   Discuss specific issues of concern.

Even if the client has not requested such a session, it is important to provide the management overview. Our experience
shows that it helps participants begin to envision what structured OJT would look like in their areas, and it gives us an
opportunity to share the experiences—both positive and
negative of other organizations.

Implementing the Pilot Study
Once the location for the pilot study has been selected, the
action plan can be carried out. The steps of the action plan
specify the sequence of events that will take place to implement structured OJT. As a rule, the steps of the action plan

combine the basic steps required for developing structured OJT as presented in this book with information that accommodates the needs of the organization.

For example, it is sometimes necessary to give various parts of the process different names to make the action plan consistent with the vocabulary used in the organization. It may also be necessary to give the steps a new sequence. For example, you may have to select and train the structured OJT trainers before you perform any of the other steps of the design process. Finally, steps sometimes have to be added to the action plan to meet the expectations of the contract. These steps can include:

❏   conducting a performance analysis
❏   preparing case studies
❏   presenting case studies to management.

To summarize, this stage of the change process combines the process presented in this book with information obtained from the organization.

Evaluating and Revising

The last step of the change process has two stages: evaluating the pilot project and making any necessary revisions.

Evaluating. As we stated in Chapter Nine, the primary purpose of evaluating structured OJT is for improvement. The evaluation is not meant to support a summative judgment on whether to keep structured OJT in place unless unforeseen events have made its continuance impossible.

We use case studies as our primary means of communicating the results of evaluation. Each case study presents all the information related to the design, implementation, and evaluation of structured OJT in a specific pilot study location. We suggest having case studies be prepared with the active participation of key stakeholders from the pilot study location. A collaborative process helps to ensure that the information presented is accurate, objective, and fair.

The case studies can be presented to stakeholders in a final written report or in an oral presentation. We always make certain that employees who helped to prepare the case studies are listed as coauthors. Case studies have proved to have a powerful effect on management decisions regarding structured OJT. They are not fabricated events; they tell the actual stories of real people within the organization.

Revising. If the case study approach is used properly, it can be extremely useful in identifying areas that need revision. In most organizations, we have several pilot study locations operating concurrently. When we have case studies for several pilot locations, they can be viewed more easily if we present them in a matrix. Across the top of the matrix, we put the names of the locations. Down the left side of the matrix, we list the structured OJT evaluation questions described in Chapter Nine. We use the evaluation data gathered from each pilot study location to complete the individual cells. The resulting display analyzes and synthesizes the entire pilot study effort. Each column in the matrix shows the evaluation results from one pilot study location. Each row compares the answers of individual locations to a single evaluation question. Distinct patterns and insights for revision can emerge when the matrix is viewed from these two perspectives.

Issues of Concern

Throughout this book, we have argued that structured OJT can enhance the performance of organizations in important ways. At this point, we need to identify and discuss some issues that can diminish its effectiveness if they are not addressed. In this section, we examine seven such issues: undue time burden, unwillingness to train, trainers' job expectations, employee development, other forms of training in the job setting, use of the deductive method, and the role of HRD staff.

Undue Time Burden

One issue that managers often express is that structured OJT places an undue time burden on employees who have already been asked to do more on the job. We find it interesting that we have heard this opinion expressed by both supervisors and frontline employees. Because job expectations have expanded, some employees have legitimate reasons for raising this issue. They can honestly feel that additional responsibilities would pose a severe hardship, even if they believe that it is worthwhile for the organization as a whole to use structured OJT.

Needless to say, we are extremely cautious about asking employees to become trainers if they are truly strained. Yet, we are skeptical until we have learned more about each situation. First, when employees initially express their views about structured OJT, almost all say that it will probably take too much of their valuable work time. Can it be true that every minute of the workday is crammed with unrelenting activity? We think not. Rather, it seems more likely that people naturally seek stability in their work lives and avoid any change, such as structured OJT, that could disrupt that stability.

Second, a trainer may become disgruntled when his or her supervisor does not provide sufficient time off to deliver structured OJT. Management needs to face the problems involved in releasing valuable employees to share their expertise with others. Long-term benefits should be carefully balanced against immediate needs. The point is that the organization should be willing to incur some reasonable costs, such as additional staffing, to allow structured OJT to occur.

Third, after delivering structured OJT several times, many employees realize that structured OJT does not interfere with their ongoing work activities as much as they had anticipated. In practice, trainers find both that structured OJT is delivered only once in a while and that it can be scheduled at mutually convenient times. In fact, some trainers—often those who voiced the loudest objections initially—look forward to the training as a way of breaking up their days and helping to make their work more interesting.

Finally, some employees who express concern about lack of time, especially supervisors, are disingenuous. Traditionally, supervisors have been expected to develop their people. Nevertheless, until recently, others within the organization have borne much of this responsibility. In many instances, the organization's human resource development staff have unwittingly taken over development activities that rightfully belong to supervisors and managers. Using structured OJT reminds supervisors that employee development is their responsibility, even if the organization has not held them accountable for it in the past.

Unwillingness to Train

The next issue of concern—the unwillingness of some experienced employees to train others—is related to the first. Overcoming this unwillingness is one of the issues most often expressed regarding structured OJT. The stubborn refusal of these individuals can be extremely frustrating for managers seeking to implement structured OJT. Unfortunately, it is virtually impossible to use structured OJT successfully without involving them.

We have two basic ways of responding to this issue. First, we say that people have reasons for their actions, although the nature of this rationality is not always clear. A person's unwillingness to train is a product of either *organization-based reasons:*

☐ Fear of a loss of status as experts
☐ Fear of threatened job security
☐ Belief that it is not part of one's job to train others
☐ Absence of incentives for doing the extra work
☐ Mistrust of management's motives

or *person-based reasons:*

☐ Discomfort in talking in front of others
☐ Uncertainty about what one knows
☐ Never having done anything like this before
☐ Lacking basic skills
☐ Nearing retirement age or will soon leave the organization for other reasons
☐ Fear of ridicule from peers.

The challenge for management is to identify the reason in the particular situation at hand and then act accordingly. In general, if the reasons are organization based, employees should at least be made aware that, if the training is successful, the performance of the group can improve. Thus, they have a stake in its success. For some employees, that is all that it takes to change their minds. In contrast, when the reasons are person based, the employee should be approached in a sensitive manner to determine whether he or she wants to address the feelings or deficiencies. Person-based reasons are usually more difficult to deal with.

Second, we question whether the issue is valid in the first place. While we have encountered individuals who were unwilling to train others, that fact has never affected the success or failure of structured OJT in their organization. If some employees do not want to train, we may find other employees who do. The fact that these other employees may be less knowledgeable in the task can be offset by the fact that they are interested in serving as trainers. In the long run, the second criterion could be more important than the first.

Our experience suggests that most employees are in fact willing to share their expertise with others. Of course, management may need to court and reassure some employees. But few employees ever refuse outright. In fact, some employees become trainers because they want to learn more about their area of expertise. For them, becoming a trainer is a way of satisfying their own learning needs. Management's expectation that employees will selfishly hoard their expertise may be no more than a reflection of more traditional, less optimistic views of employees.

Trainers' Job Expectations

In Chapter Nine, we discussed the importance of the organizational context for structured OJT. One aspect of the organizational context is management's willingness to change the job expectations of employees who serve as structured OJT trainers. It may not be possible for management to implement some changes entirely on its own initiative. For example, labor-management contracts may inhibit managers from changing job expectations without the full cooperation and agreement of their union partners. And even when changes are possible, it will doubtless take time for the changes to become a permanent part of the organization. Nevertheless, the continuing effectiveness of structured OJT depends on a thorough review of trainers' job expectations.

Consider the implications for the different categories of employees who serve as structured OJT trainers. If *supervisors or managers* are to be the trainers, then the organization should

❑ Ensure that managers have the knowledge and skills needed to deliver structured OJT

❑ Explicitly include the delivery of structured OJT in managers' job description

❑ Develop an easy-to-use system that allows managers to document and report the training progress of trainees

❑ Make the expectation to deliver training part of the performance reviews conducted by senior managers

❑ Develop a system that gives managers periodic feedback on the quality of the training that they provide.

If *frontline employees* are to be the trainers, then the organization should

❑ Ensure that employees have the knowledge and skills needed to deliver structured OJT

❑ Provide the resources needed to cover for the work missed while employees deliver training

❑ Explicitly include the delivery of structured OJT in employees' job description

❑ Develop an easy-to-use system that allows employees to document and report the training progress of trainees

❑ Develop a system that gives employees periodic feedback on the quality of the training that they provide.

These expectations are important in ensuring the quality of structured OJT.

Employee Development

Another issue that typically arises is the relationship between employee development and structured OJT. In Chapter Two, we described the four ways in which structured OJT can be used. Each way assumes that structured OJT is part of a larger employee development effort. We define *employee development* as the planned process of using training and education to help individuals to meet the organization's present and future needs (Jones & Jacobs, 1994). More and more organizations are recognizing that employee development systems are an essential part of their total quality programs. Continuous training and education opportunities help employees to make use of all their abilities and talents on the job (Vaught, Hoy, & Buchanan, 1985).

Unfortunately, structured OJT has sometimes been conducted without considering the individual needs of employees. Employees must feel that the training is moving them to a useful goal. Moreover, even when the organization has an employee development system, the system often is applied in a rather passive manner by management. That is, employees typically select training and educational experiences on their own without the guidance of a supervisor.

In more than one organization, we have found that the use of structured OJT led to the use of a more encompassing employee development system. One unanticipated effect of structured OJT is that it forces supervisors and managers to take a more active role in the development of their people.

Other Forms of Training in the Job Setting

An interesting counterpoint to structured OJT has been the growing literature on workplace training programs that seek to develop self-directedness and general problem-solving skills among trainees. De Jong (1991), whose research was conducted in the Netherlands, called this approach *on-site study.* Marsick, Cederholm, Turner, and Pearson (1992) refer to it as *action-reflection learning* (ARL). The underlying basis of these programs is that discovery learning, problem solving, and critical thinking should be the primary learning goals for trainees.

In practice, the training programs that use this approach take one of two forms: formal sessions conducted in the workplace or training embedded in the employee's job activities.

Marsick and her colleagues state that action-reflection learning programs have the following basic features:

☐ Employees work in small groups to solve problems.
☐ Employees learn to how to learn and think critically.
☐ Employees identify the skills needed to meet the requirements posed by current work.
☐ Employees develop a personal theory of management, leadership, or empowerment.

The point seems evident that views of workplace training other than structured OJT have emerged. Clearly, we do not want to have competing approaches. Each approach to workplace training seems to have its own strengths and weaknesses. Proponents of action-reflection learning suggest that it is most suitable when the problems at hand are especially complex and there is no immediate solution in sight. Creative solutions based on the learning of individual group members can be the behavioral outcomes of action-reflection learning programs. In contrast, structured OJT involves learning by individuals who seek to attain specified behavioral outcomes.

Possibly the most noticeable difference between structured OJT and action-reflection learning programs is the role of the trainer. Experienced employees are crucial in the design and delivery of structured OJT. For action-reflection learning programs, they play a different role: learning facilitator rather than source of job information. The reliance on experienced employees is said to put trainees at risk of becoming dependent on them and not seeking their own creative solutions to problems.

Clearly, structured OJT and action-reflection learning represent two fundamentally different perspectives on the training and learning process in the workplace. In a practical sense, it seems less important to determine which is superior than it does to understand both thoroughly. Each approach can make sound contributions to job and organizational performance. The linkage between organizational outcomes and action-reflection learning programs is less clear than the linkage between organizational outcomes and structured OJT.

Use of the Deductive Method

Another issue of concern is related to the issue of competing approaches. That is, structured OJT has been perceived as tied to a deductive methodology: The trainer presents the training content to the trainee, the trainee learns the content, and the trainee responds in a way that matches the presentation as closely as possible. The trainee seems to have few opportunities to internalize the content in ways other than the way in which the trainer presented it.

While the deductive method is appropriate in many training situations, it is not appropriate in all situations. In fact, the use of an inductive method or of guided discovery training is sometimes more appropriate. Resembling action-reflection learning programs in some respects, the inductive method requires the trainee to learn the content through his or her own discovery and problem-solving efforts.

In the past few years, our own interest in this issue has led us to develop new forms of structured OJT. For example, a health care organization is using structured OJT organized by the guided discovery method with newly promoted supervisors. The training program asks trainees to identify the mission of the organization, the goals of their own functional area, and the duties of a supervisor. The structured OJT is conducted by experienced supervisors or managers in the role of a facilitator. The trainer provides the training module and explains what trainees should do to achieve the training objectives. Then trainees review strategic documents and isolate specific information, interview supervisors according to a structured interview protocol, and observe supervisors in action as they do their work. They document this information in the structured OJT module. Finally, trainee and trainer review and discuss the information that has been documented. Of special importance, this training method enables trainees to identify positive and negative examples from direct observations. These personal experiences help more than the previous deductive training method to make them aware of the organization's intent and of the difficulties that employees face in carrying out that intent.

Role of HRD Staff

The last issue of concern is the proper role of HRD staff in the use of structured OJT. Clearly, there is much to do when structured OJT is used. HRD staff are uniquely suited to fulfill the following functions:

- Serve as the primary change agents by introducing structured OJT into the organization themselves or by bringing in external consultants
- Provide technical assistance in many, if not all, aspects of the structured OJT process
- Maintain files of training modules and coordinate their revision
- Coordinate the documentation of employee development plans.

Despite the many ways in which HRD staff can contribute, they still might feel left out of the process, since the structured OJT approach pushes the training process more directly onto the line side of the organization. Some HRD staff may resent that the training process seems to be out of their control. They may also be concerned that the success of structured OJT will leave senior management wondering why the organization needs an HRD department.

In a practical sense, HRD staff must not believe that their existence in the organization depends on their delivering off-the-job training programs. Instead, HRD staff must come to realize that their role is to develop employee expertise with whatever means possible. To this end, HRD staff should think of themselves broadly as system designers, not narrowly as trainers or training designers. Structured OJT has the potential to force HRD staff to reflect on what their role has been in the past and on what it should be in the future if they are to make a meaningful contribution to their organization.

Conclusion

Change management and structured OJT are two separate processes. The structured OJT process ensures that training will be designed, delivered, and evaluated in the most effective way possible. The change management process ensures that the organization will accept structured OJT. The two processes should be used in combination to ensure the successful use of structured OJT. This chapter has discussed seven issues of concern that are often raised when the use of structured OJT is considered.

C H A P T E R 11

Conclusion: Developing a Culture of Expertise

AT THIS POINT, the reader should know how to design, deliver, and evaluate structured OJT. The reader also should know that a change management process is required in order to use structured OJT successfully. This chapter concludes the book with an appeal for the development of a culture of expertise in organizations. Structured OJT would be likely to play a major role in the development of such a culture.

A Culture of Expertise

While the primary aim of this book has been to provide the reader with a practical guide to structured OJT, we believe that a reader should take away more than this information alone. As we make clear in the book's title and in Chapter One, the underlying rationale for the use of structured OJT is the need to develop employee expertise in a way that is both efficient and effective. Thus, we hope that the reader has begun to appreciate that employee expertise is a key element in an organization's success.

Managers can do many things to improve their organizations. They can bring in advanced technologies, streamline production and service delivery processes, introduce new products and services, and change work rules dramatically. But when all is said and done, what ultimately determines the success of such efforts is the abilities of individual employees.

Within the past few years, several influential writers have proposed the *learning organization* as a metaphor for the way in which organizations should undertake their own improvement and renewal (Senge, 1990; Watkins & Marsick, 1993). Of course, it is not organizations that learn but rather the people within them. The learning organization gives employees the opportunity and the license to explore their work environments fully on a continuous basis, and employees respond by accepting imposed change and initiating change on their own.

The learning organization concept is attractive to managers who are searching for a model of the type of organization that they would like to create. However, we believe that one essential element is missing from the learning organization model. Learning is important, but what can be done with the learning is even more important.

Thus, in this concluding chapter, we call on organization leaders to value the accomplishments that result from learning as much as they value learning itself. While the learning organization model has much truth, we advance the notion that what organizations need is a *culture of expertise*. For the good of both the organization and the individuals in it, employees should be encouraged to engage in continuous learning activities—but not at the expense of forgetting that learning and doing go hand in hand. On the one hand, learning by itself does not lead to enhanced productivity or improved profitability. On the other hand, expertise can be attained only through learning. Thus, having a learning organization is prerequisite to having a culture of expertise.

A culture of expertise is an environment that values what is done with learning as much as it values learning. Managers have ultimate accountability for making such an environment possible. According to Swanson and Jacobs (1994), managers can bring about a culture of expertise by taking these four steps:

1. Encourage individuals and groups to generate new areas of expertise that can help to achieve important goals.
2. Establish systems that make it possible to document and store expertise so that individuals and groups can call on it when they need it.
3. Find ways of disseminating expertise throughout the organization in ways that are both efficient and effective.
4. Remove barriers and align consequences so that individuals and groups can be recognized and even celebrated for their expertise.

Structured OJT and the Culture of Expertise

Structured OJT can play a key role in helping to make a culture of expertise possible within an organization. In the most obvious sense, structured OJT gives the organization a reliable way of disseminating important information to employees quickly and flexibly. Perhaps not so obvious are the ways in which structured OJT can make valuable contributions to other management activities.

For example, analyzing the tasks to be learned often brings insights into ways of performing a task. Training modules can be used as a way of documenting and storing task information for purposes other than training. Finally, an organization can recognize experienced employees who serve as structured OJT trainers. All these contributions give structured OJT a key role in the culture of expertise. Viewed from this perspective, structured OJT can be seen as helping an organization to start the process of becoming a learning organization in the truest sense of the word, since it gives the organization a way of sharing old and new expertise effectively and efficiently with all employees.

Conclusion

Organizations in the new economy have come to realize that employee expertise is a vital and dynamic living treasure. The desire for employee expertise is meaningless unless an organization can develop it in ways that respond to its business needs. Structured OJT is one proven way of developing employee expertise that helps an organization to meet the changing needs of today's competitive marketplace.

REFERENCES

Ausubel, D. P. (1968). *Educational psychology: A cognitive view.* New York: Holt, Rinehart & Winston.

Baldwin, T. T., and Ford, K. J. (1988). Transfer of training: A review and directions for future research. *Personnel Psychology, 41*(1), 63–105.

Bandura, A. (1978). *Social learning theory.* Englewood Cliffs, NJ: Prentice-Hall.

Black, D., and Bottenberg, R. A. (1973). *Comparison of technical school and on-the-job training as methods of skill upgrading.* San Antonio, TX: Air Force Human Resources Laboratory.

Bloom, B. S. (1984). The 2-sigma problem: The search for methods of group instruction as effective as one-on-one tutoring. *Educational Researcher, 13*(6), 4–16.

Brinkerhoff, R. O. (1987). *Achieving results from training: How to evaluate human resource development to strengthen programs and increase impact.* San Francisco: Jossey-Bass.

Broad, M. L., and Newstrom, J. W. (1992). *Transfer of training: Action-packed strategies to ensure higher payoffs from training investments.* Reading, MA: Addison-Wesley.

Broadwell, M. M. (1986). *The supervisor and on-the-job training.* Reading, MA: Addison-Wesley.

Brown, J. S., Collins, A., and Duguid, P. (1989). Situated cognition and the culture of learning. *Educational Researcher, 18*(1), 32–41.

Carlisle, K. E. (1986). *Analyzing jobs and tasks.* Englewood Cliffs, NJ: Educational Technology Publications.

Carnevale, A. P. (1991). *America and the new economy.* Alexandria, VA: American Society for Training and Development and Employment Training Administration, U.S. Department of Labor.

Carnevale, A. P., and Carnevale, E. S. (1994, May/June). Trends in training on the job. *Technical and Skills Training,* 10–16.

Carnevale, A. P., and Gainer, L. J. (1989). *The learning enterprise.* Alexandria, VA: American Society for Training and Development and Employment and Training Administration, U.S. Department of Labor.

Chi, M. T., Glaser, R., and Farr, M. J. (1988). *The nature of expertise.* Hillsdale, NJ: Erlbaum.

Churchill, G. A., Ford, N. M., and Walker, O. C. (1985). *Sales force management: Planning, implementation, and control.* Homewood, IL: Irwin.

Connor, J. (1983). *On-the-job training.* Boston: International Human Resources Development Corporation.

Cronbach, L. J., and Snow, R. E. (1977). *Aptitudes and instructional methods.* New York: Irvington.

Cummings, T. G., and Worley, C. G. (1993). *Organization development and change.* St. Paul, MN: West.

De Jong, J. A. (1991). The multiple forms of on-site training. *Human Resource Development Quarterly, 2*(4), 307–317.

De Jong, J. A. (1993) Structured on-the-job training at Hoogovens Ijmuiden. *Journal of European Industrial Training, 17*(2), 8–13.

Dixon, N. M. (1990). *Evaluation: A tool for improving HRD quality.* San Diego, CA: University Associates.

Dooley, C. R. (1945). *The Training Within Industry report (1940–1945): A record of the development of management techniques for improvement of supervision—their use and the results.* War Manpower Commission, Bureau of Training, Training Within Industry Service.

Dowling, N. (1992). *The relationship between senior managers' quality management behaviors and subordinate managers' commitment to quality.* Unpublished doctoral dissertation, Ohio State University.

Drucker, P. (1993). *Post-capitalist society.* New York: Harper-Collins.

Fournies, F. F. (1978). *Coaching for improved work performance.* New York: Van Nostrand Reinhold.

Futrell, C. (1988). *Sales management.* Hinsdale, IL: Dryden Press.

Gagne, R. M., Briggs, L. J., and Wager, W. W. (1988). *Principles of instructional design.* New York: Holt, Rinehart & Winston.

Gilbert, T. F. (1978). *Human competence: Engineering worthy performance.* New York: McGraw-Hill.

Goldstein, I. (1974). *Training program development.* Monterey, CA: Brooks/Cole.

Gommersall, E., and Meyers, M. S. (1966). Breakthrough in on-the-job training. *Harvard Business Review, 44*(4), 62–72.

Harless, J. H. (1978). *An ounce of analysis is worth a pound of objectives.* Newnan, GA: Harless Performance Guild.

Hartley, J., and Davies, I. K. (1976). Preinstructional strategies: The role of pretests, behavioral objectives, overviews, and advance organizers. *Review of Educational Research, 46*(2), 239–265.

Hart-Landsberg, S., Braunger, J., Reder, S., and Cross, M. M. (1992). *Learning the ropes: The social construction of work-based learning.* Berkeley, CA: National Center for Research in Vocational Education.

Jacobs, R. L. (1986). Use of the critical incident technique to analyze the interpersonal skill requirements of supervisors. *Journal of Industrial Teacher Education, 23*(2), 56–61.

Jacobs, R. L. (1989). Systems theory applied to human resource development. In D. Gradous (ed.), *Systems theory applied to human resource development.* Alexandria, VA: American Society for Training and Development.

Jacobs, R. L. (1990). Structured on-the-job training. In H. Stolovitch and E. Keeps (eds.), *Handbook of human performance technology: A comprehensive guide for analyzing and solving performance problems in organizations.* San Francisco: Jossey-Bass.

Jacobs, R. L. (1994). Comparing the training efficiency and product quality of unstructured and structured OJT. In J. Phillips (ed.), *The return on investment in human resource development: Cases on the economic benefits of HRD.* Alexandria, VA: American Society for Training and Development.

Jacobs, R. L., Jones, M. J., and Neil, S. (1992). A case study in forecasting the financial benefits of unstructured and structured on-the-job training. *Human Resource Development Quarterly, 3*(2), 133–139.

Jacobs, R. L., and McGiffin, T. D. (1987). A human performance system using a structured on-the-job training approach. *Performance and Instruction, 25*(7), 8–11.

Johnston, W. B., and Packer, A. H. (1987). *Workforce 2000: Work and workers for the 21st century.* Indianapolis, IN: Hudson Institute.

Jonassen, D. H. (ed.). (1982). *The technology of text: Principles for structuring, designing, and displaying text.* Englewood Cliffs, NJ: Educational Technology Publications.

Jonassen, D. H., Hannum, W. H., and Tessmer, M. (1989) *Handbook of task analysis procedures.* New York: Praeger.

Jones, M. J., and Jacobs, R. L. (1994). Developing frontline employees: New challenges for achieving organizational effectiveness. In R. Kaufman and T. Sivasailam (eds.), *Handbook of human performance systems.* San Diego, CA: University Associates.

Kainen, T. L., Begley, T. M., and Maggard, M. J. (1983). On-the-job training and work unit performance. *Training and Development Journal, 37*(4), 84–87.

Kaufman, R., and Jones, M. J. (1990). The industrial survival of the nation: Union-management cooperation. *Human Resource Development Quarterly, 1*(1), 87–91.

Kaufman, R., and Zahn, D. (1993). *Quality management plus: The continuous improvement of education.* Newbury Park, CA: Corwin Press.

Kirkpatrick, D. L. (1985). Effective supervisory training and development, Part 2: In-house approaches and techniques. *Personnel, 62*(1), 52–56.

Kondrasuk, J. (1979). The best way to train managers... *Training and Development Journal, 33*(8), 46–48.

Kotter, J., and Heskett, J. (1992). *Corporate culture and performance.* Cambridge, MA: Harvard University Press.

Lave, J., and Wenger, E. (1991). *Situated learning: Legitimate peripheral participation.* Port Chester, NY: Cambridge University Press.

Leach, J. A. (1991). Characteristics of excellent trainers: A psychological and interpersonal profile. *Performance and Instruction Quarterly, 4*(3), 42–62.

McCord, A. (1987). Job training. In R. L. Craig (ed.), *Training and development handbook: A guide to human resource development.* New York: McGraw-Hill.

Mager, R. F. (1984). *Preparing instructional objectives.* Belmont, CA: Fearon.

Mangum, S. (1985). On-the-job vs. classroom training: Some deciding factors. *Training, 22*(2), 75–77.

Marsick, V. J. (1988). Learning in the workplace: The case for reflectivity and critical reflectivity. *Adult Education Quarterly, 38*(4), 187–198.

Marsick, V. J., Cederholm, L., Turner, E., and Pearson, T. (1992, August). Action-reflection learning. *Training and Development,* pp. 63–66.

Martin, B. J. (1991, October). A system for on-the-job training. *Technical and Skills Training, 2*(7), 24–28.

Miller, V. A. (1987). The history of training. In R. L. Craig (ed.), *Training and development handbook: A guide to human resource development.* New York: McGraw-Hill.

Powers, B. (1992). *Instructor excellence: Mastering the delivery of training.* San Francisco: Jossey-Bass.

Robinson, D. G., and Robinson, J. C. (1989). *Training for impact: How to link training to business needs and measure results.* San Francisco: Jossey-Bass.

Rossett, A. (1987). *Training needs assessment.* Englewood Cliffs, NJ: Educational Technology Publications.

Rossett, A., and Gautier-Downes, J. (1991). *A handbook of job aids.* San Diego, CA: Pfeiffer.

Rothwell, W., and Kazanas, H. (1990). Structured on-the-job training (SOJT) as perceived by HRD professionals. *Performance Improvement Quarterly, 3*(3), 12–26.

Rummler, G. A., and Brache, A. P. (1990). *Improving performance: How to manage the white space on the organization chart.* San Francisco: Jossey-Bass.

Senge, P. M. (1990). *The fifth discipline: The art and practice of the learning organization.* New York: Doubleday.

Shrock, S., and Coscarelli, W. (1989). *Criterion-referenced test development.* Reading, MA: Addison-Wesley.

Sloman, M. (1989, February). On-the-job training: A costly poor relation. *Personnel Management, 21*(2), 38–41.

Stokes, P. M. (1966). *Total job training: A manual for the working manager.* Washington, D.C. : American Management Association.

Sullivan, R. F., and Miklas, D. C. (1985). On-the-job training that works. *Training and Development Journal, 39*(5), 118–120.

Swanson, R. A. (1994). *Analysis for improving performance: Tools for diagnosing organizations and documenting workplace expertise.* San Francisco: Berrett-Koehler.

Swanson, R. A., and Gradous, D. (1988). *Forecasting the financial benefits of human resource development programs.* San Francisco: Jossey-Bass.

Swanson, R. A., and Jacobs, R. L. (1994). System components of an organizational culture of employee expertise. Unpublished manuscript, Ohio State University.

Swanson, R. A., and Law, B. D. (1993). Whole-part-whole learning model. *Performance Improvement Quarterly, 6*(1), 43–53.

Swanson, R. A., and Sawzin, S. A. (1975). *Industrial training research project.* Bowling Green, OH: Bowling Green State University.

Tiemann, P. W., and Markle, S. M. (1983). *Analyzing instructional content: A guide to instruction and evaluation.* Champaign, IL: Stipes.

Tracey, W. R. (1974). *Managing training and development systems.* New York: AMACON.

Utgaard, S. B., and Davis, R. V. (1970). The most frequently used training techniques. *Training and Development Journal, 24*(2), 40–43.

Vaught, B. C., Hoy, F., and Buchanan, W. W. (1985). Employee development programs: An organizational approach. Westport, CT: Quorum Books.

Von Bertalanffy, L. (1968). *General systems theory: Foundations, development, applications.* New York: Braziller.

Watkins, K., and Marsick, V. J. (1993). Sculpting the learning organization: Lessons in the art and science of systemic change. San Francisco: Jossey-Bass.

Wehrenberg, S. B. (1987). Supervisors as trainers: The long-term gains of OJT. *Personnel Journal, 66*(4), 48–51.

Westgaard, O. (1993). *Good fair tests for use in business and industry.* Amherst, MA: HRD Press.

Wexley, K. (1988). A tale of two problems: On-the-job training and positive transfer. In R. Schuler, S. Youngblood, and V. Huber (eds.), *Readings in personnel and human resource management.* St. Paul, MN: West.

Wexley, K. N., and Latham, G. P. (1991). Developing and training human resources in organizations. New York: HarperCollins.

Wichman, M. A. (1989). On-the-job training: Formalizing informality or shouldn't supervisors do the training? *Performance and Instruction, 28*(1), 31–32.

Zemke, R., and Kramlinger, T. (1984). *Figuring things out: A trainer's guide to needs and task analysis.* Reading, MA: Addison-Wesley.

INDEX

The Authors

RONALD L. JACOBS, associate professor of human resource development at the Ohio State University, earned his B.F.A. degree in film studies and English from Ohio University, his M.A. degree in educational technology from the University of Toledo, and his Ph.D. degree in instructional systems technology from Indiana University. Before joining the faculty of the Ohio State University, Jacobs was a faculty member at Southern Illinois University, Carbondale.

Past chair of the National Research Committee of the American Society for Training and Development, Jacobs is vice president for research of the Academy of Human Resource Development. Associate editor of *Human Resource Development Quarterly,* he has served on the editorial boards of *Performance and Instruction, Performance Improvement Quarterly,* and the *Journal of Industrial Teacher Education.*

Author of the ERIC monograph *Human Performance Technology: A Proposed Framework for the Training and Development Profession* and editor of *Organizational Issues and Human Resource Development Research Questions,* Jacobs has authored or coauthored more than seventy-five journal articles and book chapters.

Jacobs has consulted with organizations in the areas of training design, organization development, and process improvement. In the past ten years, much of his research and consulting activity has focused on structured OJT. He has given numerous presentations and consulted with organizations in Taiwan, Egypt, and the Netherlands.

MICHAEL J. JONES, an experienced practitioner, is manager of human resource development in a large production company. He earned his B.S. degree in secondary education and his M.A. degree in human resource development from the Ohio State University. His business experience includes fifteen years managing training in the automotive industries. He is an adjunct professor of human resource management at Ohio University.

Jones has coauthored articles and book chapters on structured OJT, employee development, and organizational change in the new economy. A member of the National Society for Performance and Instruction (NSPI), Jones is past president of the Heartland Central Ohio Chapter of the NSPI. He has made presentations at numerous national conferences, including the American Society for Training and Development's Technical Skills Conference and the National Society for Performance and Instruction.